Everything Voluntary
From Politics to Parenting

Edited by Skyler J. Collins
Foreword by Chris R. Brown, PhD

Everything Voluntary
From Politics to Parenting

Editor

Skyler J. Collins

Foreword

Chris R. Brown, PhD

Contributors

Alice Miller
Carl Watner
Daniel Quinn
David J. Theroux
Donald J. Boudreaux
Earl Stevens
Hans-Hermann Hoppe
Henry Hazlitt
James Kimmell
James Luther Adams
Jan Hunt
Jason Hunt
John D. Fargo
John Holt

Karl H. Meyer
Leonard E. Read
Mark & Jo Ann Skousen
Marshall B. Rosenberg
Missy Willis
Murray N. Rothbard
Nicholas Hooton
Pam Laricchia
Richard Ebeling
Robin Grille
Sandra Dodd
Vahram G. Diehl
Wendy McElroy

www.everything-voluntary.com

Salt Lake City, Utah

Published 2012 by Skyler J. Collins
Visit: www.skylerjcollins.com

"V for Voluntary" symbol created by Niels van der Linden, 2007.
Visit: www.vforvoluntary.com

ISBN–13: 978-1477419892
ISBN–10: 1477419896

BISAC: Philosophy / Ethics & Moral Philosophy

*To humankind
and our posterity.*

Table of Contents

Foreword by *Chris R. Brown, PhD*..xi
Preface xiii
Introduction 17

Section One – Politics

1 – Persuasion versus Force... 25
    by Mark & Jo Ann Skousen
2 – Coercivists and Voluntarists... 35
    by Donald J. Boudreaux
3 – Fundamentals of Voluntaryism.. 39
    by Carl Watner
4 – The Anatomy of the State 44
    by Murray N. Rothbard
5 – Thoughts on Nonviolence..67
    by Karl H. Meyer
6 – Charity in the Land of Individualism.. 70
    by John D. Fargo

Voluntaryist Resources 74

Section Two – Religion

7 – The Origin of Religious Tolerance..81
    by Wendy McElroy
8 – The Historical Origins of Voluntaryism... 87
    by James Luther Adams
9 – For Conscience's Sake... 90
    by Carl Watner
10 – Secular Theocracy 103
    by David J. Theroux

Section Three – Economy

11 – I, Pencil.. 115
    by Leonard E. Reed
12 – What is the Free Market?..122
    by Murray N. Rothbard
13 – Planning vs. the Free Market..128
    by Henry Hazlitt
14 – Historical Capitalism vs. the Free Market.....................................139
    by Richard Ebeling
15 – Why Socialism Must Fail..144
    by Hans-Hermann Hoppe
16 – Agorist Living 150
    by Nicholas Hooton

Free Market Resources 156

Section Four – Education

17 – The Trouble with Traditional Schooling 163
by *Vahram G. Diehl*
18 – Schooling: The Hidden Agenda....................... 167
by *Daniel Quinn*
19 – The Right to Control One's Learning 179
by *John Holt*
20 – What is Unschooling? 185
by *Earl Stevens*
21 – Whose Goal is it, Anyway?....................... 191
by *Pam Laricchia*
22 – Unexpected Benefits of Unschooling....................... 199
by *Sandra Dodd*
23 – Grown Without Schooling....................... 208
by *Jason Hunt*

Unschooling Resources 212

Section Five – Parenting

24 – Natural Born Bullies....................... 219
by *Robin Grille*
25 – Childhood: The Unexplored Source of Knowledge 225
by *Alice Miller*
26 – Why Do We Hurt Our Children? 237
by *James Kimmell*
27 – On Seeing Children as "Cute"....................... 252
by *John Holt*
28 – 10 Ways We Misunderstand Children....................... 259
by *Jan Hunt*
29 – Raising Children Compassionately....................... 262
by *Marshall B. Rosenberg*
30 – Born to Explore 272
by *Missy Willis*

Parenting Resources 276

Afterword 281
Topical Guide 284
About the Editor 285

Foreword

Voluntaryism is a simple concept and one many people agree with superficially. Ask most people if they believe in forcing an individual to act according to another's whim and they are likely to say "No." "Live and let live," or "Do unto others as you would have them do unto you" – the Golden Rule – are common aphorisms that communicate voluntaryism. So, if most individuals agree with the Golden Rule, why aren't we all voluntaryists?

This book will show you why. Voluntaryists take the Golden Rule very seriously and apply it to everyone, regardless of status or role, whether teacher, parent, ecclesiastical, professional, or governmental leader. Thus, confusion arises not primarily from misunderstanding the principles supporting voluntaryism – private property and the non-aggression axiom – but in how to apply those principles to the wide and complicated variety of situations found in everyday experience.

In this volume, Skyler unravels that complexity by his inclusion of key articles that apply voluntaryism to Politics, Religion, Economy, Education, and Family. These are foundational areas that not only affect everyone, but are also extensively influenced by the state, with its monopoly on the use of force. This work represents both introduction and depth to the philosophy of voluntaryism.

I have observed Skyler's intellectual engagement with topics dealing with liberty over the last few years. He is constantly absorbing, digesting and synthesizing a wide range of materials to better grasp new ideas and concepts in this domain. I expect this volume is the beginning of what will be many books that Skyler puts forth.

- Chris R. Brown, PhD

Preface

If I may take a personal route, this book is the culmination of the last 7 years of my academic life. It's been quite the intellectual journey. I've evolved from a progressive liberal to a free-market conservative to a *laissez faire* libertarian, and finally, a voluntaryist (or voluntarist). Of course, it wasn't until very recently that my focus turned toward my parenting. I certainly didn't approach my children as a voluntaryist. More like a barbarian.

The pieces finally fit when I was introduced to Alfie Kohn's *Unconditional Parenting* by a very good friend of mine, a mentor, and author of my foreword, Chris Brown. As my wife and I implemented his philosophy, it became obvious that sending our children to public school would most likely reverse everything we wanted to accomplish. The schools still reward good behavior and punish bad (as if children can "misbehave"). Well-meaning teachers would raise our children in ways that we believe are unhealthy for them as individuals and as human beings.

I had read a little about a homeschooling philosophy called "unschooling" a year prior, when our son first started preschool. With our recent change in parenting style, and realization that school would hinder our efforts, I jumped online to find out more about this unschooling. I was quickly "converted" and managed to convince my wife to give it a go.

My son would be in Kindergarten right now, but instead is discovering all sorts of amazing things via museums, recreational activities, books, television, the Internet, and video games, i.e., *the world*. He insists on asking my wife and me a thousand questions about every little thing he's discovered, every chance he gets. It can be very tiring those days I'm not in the mood (I work multiple jobs, you see), and he's learning to trust me when I tell him that I need some quiet time. He knows it'll be short order before we can have another conversation about whatever it is that's caught his interest.

His first year's almost up (that is if we can still call it that), and our relationships with both of our children are simply amazing. Our home boasts the complete absence of violence. Sure my kids (my son is 6½ and my daughter is 2½ as of this writing) tussle from time to time, but they're getting very good at working it out, and their relationship is wonderful. They adore each other.

In November of last year, I decided to launch a blog that would focus on "everything voluntary." Politics, the market, parenting, education, all of it; if it was based on mutual consent, I wanted to promote protecting it, and if not, then I wanted to bury it. It has no place in the civilized world, and sure as heck has no place in the home!

When I set out to put together a book on these topics, a voluntaryist primer, I soon questioned my approach. I thought, "Why reinvent the wheel?" I had already discovered so many gems on my journey these last 7 years; why not just put them all together under different sections, introducing the reader to the voluntaryist argument? Others have said it better than I could, anyway. Why not climb up onto the shoulders of giants and merely bring attention to them?

Other books on voluntaryism focused on politics, the market, and homeschooling in general. I wanted this one to focus more on the parent/child relationship and on childhood development, where I believe liberty will be saved, within our families. (It came out to about half dealing with the outside world and half in the home.)

That became the plan, as did self-publishing my book. I wanted complete control over the content. As far as that's concerned, this is a bit of an experiment. I've never self-published a book before, nor have I ever edited, formatted, typeset, or marketed one. Now I have. It's been incredibly fun, and I've got plans for more! I hope you enjoy it, and I hope you pay attention to my admonitions in the Afterword.

Acknowledgements

I would like to extend a gigantic heartfelt "thank you" to Jan Hunt and her Natural Child Project (naturalchild.org). She provided me a considerable amount of aid in gathering permissions to reprint several essays found via the Project. Her website is a wonderful collection of some of the best essays and books I've discovered on peaceful parenting and childhood learning. Please visit the Project and if you like what you see, consider making a donation.

A special "thank you" also goes out to the following individuals for their assistance: Chris Brown, Nic Hooton, Spencer Morgan, Mark Skousen, Jesse Thomas, Wes Bertrand, Lou Gignac, Vahram Diehl, and to all of my contributors, whose work has been an invaluable source of wisdom for me and millions of others.

Saving the best for last, "thank you" to my beautiful and wonderful wife Julieta, for the amazing children she has given me, and for her much needed love and support. Nobody can compare to the companion she has been on this wild ride we call our life.

Technical Note

I also want to make it clear that one contributor's opinion is not necessarily the opinion of every other contributor. Their ideas are their own.

- Skyler J. Collins, Editor

Introduction
Skyler J. Collins, Editor

The mainstream political, education, and parenting philosophies all have one thing in common: promoting the domination of one group of people over another. In politics, this is the ruling class, i.e., politicians and bureaucrats, over the ruled. In education and parenting, this is teachers or parents over their children. Someone's interest prevails over someone else's, and in these arenas, *violent* solutions prevail over peaceful ones.

The purpose of this book is to question the "virtues" of human relations based on violent coercion, and to promote instead human relations based on mutual consent. For it is under one type or the other that human interaction in all arenas of life necessarily fall.

From large-scale social organization and maintenance to the small-scale family unit, it is the position of this editor that peace and prosperity are most likely achieved through relations based on mutual consent. This book should prime the reader to develop an understanding and commitment to the political, social, and life philosophy called "voluntaryism."

Voluntaryism evolved from libertarianism and its two foundational principles: the *self-ownership of every individual* and the *non-initiation of aggression*. The complete recognition and total utilization of these principles in not only politics and law, but also in the economy, education, and parenting, is voluntaryism. Peace and prosperity are the ends, voluntaryism is the *only* means.

This book is a compilation of essays carefully selected by the editor to introduce the reader to voluntaryism specifically, and libertarianism generally. They are a mixture of classic and modern from varied writers who all have at least one thing in common: their commitment to voluntary action in their area of expertise.

Politics

We begin this primer with the widest view of human life on Earth. The political arena the world over is rife with conflicts and contentions. No matter the system of government, be it a monarchy, a democracy, constitutional, or totalitarian, they all rely on the use of violent coercion to create benefits for one group or groups of people forcibly derived from another. Kings and lords over serfs and subjects; the majority over the minority; representatives and special interests over citizens; a dictator and his army over slaves.

Where is the system of governance that relies on persuasion instead of force? Can a system of governance be realized without one group's interests taking forceful precedent over another's? Is a "system" of governance even necessary? Should government be centrally planned by "the elite", or decentrally developed by "the people"? What is the alternative to the so-called "necessary evil" of the State? What is the alternative to what amounts to the enslavement of mankind?

Religion

Throughout the history of the world, people have co-opted the State in order to spread their religious ideas "by the sword." Religions were held up, funded by, and protected by violence. Religious intolerance was everywhere, and, unfortunately, is still found in many places today. When and how did religious *tolerance* develop? What was it that brought people of different religious beliefs together to work out the problems of mutual existence?

One of the greatest triumphs of liberty was the spread of the doctrine of "separation of Church and State." In most nations of the world one can follow his conscience and worship whoever or whatever he pleases, so long as his worship does not violate anyone else's rights to do likewise. Even non-believers are protected by this beautiful doctrine of religious peace.

But not so fast. While official religion has been mostly removed from the "public sphere," another more insidious institution has taken its place as the object of zealous devotion. With temples, oaths, hymns, covenants, banners, and liturgical practices, the State has made for itself a religion all its own. Society now tolerates different views on God, but question one's Nation, and you'll invite for yourself some serious trouble. If you want to see how bitter people can become, refuse to salute the national banner, recite the national covenant of allegiance, or sing the national hymns, and you shortly will. Their cult-like commitment to the State becomes painfully obvious. Secular theocracy now rules the world over.

Economy

On to the most important sphere of life to the typical human being. How an economy is structured can mean abundance and plenty, or scarcity and death. Should people be free to trade their property and their services unmolested? Or should the State intervene to control the market with regulations, price controls, professional licensure, and paper money?

The 16th and 17th centuries saw the birth of free market economics. The 18th and 19th centuries saw its realization, mostly, and the biggest advancements in industry and the standard of living the world had ever seen. They also saw the birth of Socialism, and the 20th century saw Socialism's *bloody* realization.

However, the 20th century also saw the near-death and rebirth of a particular strand of free market economics, the so-called Austrian School. Named after its greatest pioneers, Austrians Carl Menger, Eugen von

Bohm-Bawerk, and Ludwig von Mises, the Austrian School of economics is the greatest and most consistent school of free market economic thought. It is from this school that we will explore both the free market and its alternative, for only this school is completely compatible with peace, prosperity, and voluntaryism.

Education

Our second half of the book, the last two sections, brings us into our homes and families. Our children are literally the future of humankind. The State knows this, and has gone to significant lengths to undermine and replace the parental role. Its biggest success is in compulsory schooling. In most of the world, children are forced by the State to go to school. Where they aren't, parents forcibly educate their children at home. Absent are the rights and will of the child toward his own education.

Fortunately, there is an alternative: *unschooling*. After revealing the hidden agendas of compulsory schooling, we'll explore the curious and extraordinary world of unschooling. For only unschooling is compatible with the principles of voluntaryism. True unschooling, however, is not only limited to a child's academics. It's concerned with the entire parent-child relationship. This brings us to our final section.

Parenting

The home is where the bedrock of freedom must be laid, and the seeds of liberty planted, and cultivated by parents committed to the future peace and prosperity of their children. It's also where children learn how to become functional adults. How parents treat their children teaches children a great deal about human relations. This point cannot be stressed enough. From infancy onward, how children are treated makes the difference between an Adolf Hitler and a Mother Teresa. There is no excuse for violence in the home, where children are born with an expectation of love and safety.

Parents that are mean and violent show children how to be mean and violent towards other human beings, and when these children do as they're shown, they're labeled as bullies and deviants. On the other hand, parents who approach their children as fellow human beings, having dignity, deserving respect, and acknowledged as simply ignorant about life are instead peacefully mentored through life's many challenges. Children are easily misunderstood, and parents are quick to set unreasonable expectations for their children. This leads to conflict and heartache instead of peace and love. We shall peak into the world of voluntaryist parenting, where children are raised with love and compassion, instead of fear and violence.

Resources

This brings us to the end of this introduction. Each of the topics above are given due consideration within this book, however, what is herein presented is merely the *tip* of the proverbial iceberg. It's what's under the water that is truly fascinating and life changing. For that, each section (besides Religion) is followed by a short compilation of resources, both in print and on the Internet. These resources represent the best of what this editor has discovered. Their importance in developing one's understanding of voluntaryism, free market economics, unschooling, and peaceful parenting cannot be understated. The future of humankind is quite literally at stake. This book is dedicated to that future. Godspeed!

Section One – Politics

1
Persuasion versus Force
by Mark & Jo Ann Skousen

Sometimes a single book or even a short cogent essay can change an individual's entire outlook on life. For Christians, it is the *New Testament*. For radical socialists, Karl Marx' and Friedrich Engels' *The Communist Manifesto* is revolutionary. For libertarians, Ayn Rand's *Atlas Shrugged* is pivotal. For economists, Ludwig von Mises' *Human Action* can be mind-changing.

Recently I came across a little essay in a book called *Adventures of Ideas*, by Alfred North Whitehead, the British philosopher and Harvard professor. The essay, "From Force to Persuasion," had a profound effect upon me. Actually, what caught my attention was a single passage on page 83. This one small excerpt in a 300-page book changed my entire political philosophy.

Here's what it says:

> "The creation of the world – said Plato – is the victory of persuasion over force... Civilization is the maintenance of social order, by its own inherent persuasiveness as embodying the nobler

alternative. The recourse to force, however unavoidable, is a disclosure of the failure of civilization, either in the general society or in a remnant of individuals…

"Now the intercourse between individuals and between social groups takes one of these two forms: force or persuasion. Commerce is the great example of intercourse by way of persuasion. War, slavery, and governmental compulsion exemplify the reign of force."

Professor Whitehead's vision of civilized society as the triumph of persuasion over force should become paramount in the mind of all civic-minded individuals and government leaders. It should serve as the guideline for the political ideal.

Let me suggest, therefore, a new political creed: The triumph of persuasion over force is the sign of a civilized society.

Surely this is a fundamental principle to which most citizens, no matter where they fit on the political spectrum, can agree.

Too Many Laws

Too often lawmakers resort to the force of law rather than the power of persuasion to solve a problem in society. They are too quick to pass another statute or regulation in an effort to suppress the effects of a deep-rooted problem in society rather than seeking to recognize and deal with the real cause of the problem, which may require parents, teachers, pastors, and community leaders to convince people to change their ways.

Too often politicians think that new programs requiring new taxes are the only way to pay for citizens' retirement, health care, education or other social needs. "People just aren't willing to pay for these services themselves," they say, so they force others to pay for them instead.

Supreme Court Justice Oliver Wendell Holmes once said, "Taxation is the price we pay for civilization." But isn't the opposite really the case? Taxation is the price we pay for failing to build a civilized society. The higher the tax level, the greater the failure. A centrally planned totalitarian state represents a complete defeat for the civilized world, while a totally voluntary society represents its ultimate success.

Thus, legislators, ostensibly concerned about poverty and low wages, pass a minimum wage law and establish a welfare state as their way to abolish poverty. Yet poverty persists, not for want of money, but for want of skills, capital, education, and the desire to succeed.

The community demands a complete education for all children, so the state mandates that all children attend school for at least ten years. Winter Park High School, which two of our children attend, is completely fenced in. Students need a written excuse to leave school grounds and an official explanation for absences. All the gates except one are closed during school hours, and there is a permanent guard placed at the only open gate to monitor students coming and going. Florida recently passed a law that takes away the driver's license of any student who drops out of high school. Surely, they say, that will eliminate the high drop-out rate for students.

But suppressing one problem only creates another. Now students who don't want to be in school are disrupting the students who want to learn. The lawmakers forget one thing. Schooling is not the same as education.

Many high-minded citizens don't like to see racial, religious or sexual discrimination in employment, housing, department stores, restaurants, and clubs. Yet instead of persuading people in the schools, the churches, and the media that discrimination is inappropriate behavior and morally repugnant, law-makers simply pass civil rights legislation outlawing discrimination, as though making hatred illegal can instantly make it go away. Instead, forced integration often intensifies the already-existing hostilities. Does anyone wonder why discrimination is still a serious problem in our society?

Is competition from the Japanese, the Germans and the Brazilians too stiff for American industry? We can solve that right away, says Congress. No use trying to convince industry to invest in more productive labor and capital, or voting to reduce the tax burden on business. No, they'll just impose import quotas or heavy duties on foreign products and force them to "play fair." Surely that will make us more competitive, and keep American companies in business.

Drugs, Guns, and Abortion

Is the use of mind-altering drugs a problem in America? Then let's pass legislation prohibiting the use of certain high-powered drugs. People still want to use them? Then let's hire more police to crack down on the drug users and drug dealers. Surely that will solve the problem. Yet such laws never address the fundamental issue, which would require analyzing why people misuse drugs and discovering ways they can satisfy their needs in a nondestructive manner. By out-lawing illicit drugs, we fail to consider the underlying cause of increased drug or alcohol misuse among teenagers and adults, and we fail to accept the beneficial uses of such drugs in medicine and health-care. I salute voluntary efforts in communities to deal with these serious problems, such as "no alcohol" high school graduation parties and drug-awareness classes. Tobacco is on the decline as a result of education, and drug use could abate as well if it were treated as a medical problem rather than a criminal one.

Abortion is a troublesome issue, we all agree on that. Whose rights take precedence, the baby's or the mother's? When does life begin, at conception or at birth?

Political conservatives are shocked by the millions of legal killings that take place every year in America and around the world. How can we sing "God Bless America" with this epidemic plaguing our nation? So, for many conservatives the answer is simple: Ban abortions! Force women to give birth to their unexpected and unwanted babies. That will solve the problem. This quick fix will undoubtedly give the appearance that we have instantly solved our national penchant for genocide.

Wouldn't it be better if we first tried to answer the all important questions, "Why is abortion so prevalent today, and how can we prevent unwanted pregnancies?" Or, once an unwanted pregnancy occurs, how can we persuade people to examine alternatives, including adoption?

Crime is another issue plaguing this country. There are those in society who want to ban handguns, rifles and other firearms, or at least have them tightly controlled and registered, in an attempt to reduce crime. We can solve the murder and crime problem in this country, they reason, simply by passing a law taking away the weapons of murder. No guns, no killings. Simple, right? Yet they only change the outward symptoms, while showing little interest in finding ways to discourage a person from becoming criminal or violent in the first place.

Legislators should be slow to pass laws to protect people against themselves. While insisting on a woman's "right to choose" in one area, they deny men and women the right to choose in every other area. Unfortunately, they are all too quick to act. Drivers aren't wearing their seatbelts? Let's pass a mandatory seatbelt law. Motorcyclists aren't wearing helmets? Let's mandate helmets. We'll force people to be responsible!

More Than Just Freedom

How did we get into this situation, where lawmakers feel compelled to legislate personal behavior "for our own good"? Often we only have ourselves to blame.

The lesson is clear: If we are going to preserve what personal and economic freedom we have left in this country, we had better act responsibly, or our freedom is going to be taken away. Too many detractors think that freedom is nothing more than the right to act irresponsibly. They equate liberty with libertine behavior: that the freedom to choose whether to have an abortion means that they should have an abortion, that the freedom to take drugs means that they should take drugs, that the legalization of gambling means that they should play the roulette wheel.

It is significant that Professor Whitehead chose the word "persuasion," not simply "freedom," as the ideal characteristic of the civilized world. The word "persuasion" embodies both freedom of choice and responsibility for choice. In order to persuade, you must have a moral philosophy, a system of right and wrong, with which you govern yourself. You want to persuade people to do the right thing not because they have to, but because they want to.

There is little satisfaction from doing good if individuals are mandated to do the right thing. Character and responsibility are built when people voluntarily choose right over wrong, not when they are forced to do so. A soldier will feel a greater sense of victory if he enlists in the armed forces instead of being drafted. And high school students will not comprehend the joy of service if it is mandated by a community-service requirement for graduation.

Admittedly, there will be individuals in a free society who will make the wrong choices, who will become drug addicts and alcoholics, who will refuse to wear a safety helmet, who will hurt themselves playing with firecrackers, and who will drop out of high school. But that is the price we must pay for having a free society, where individuals learn from their mistakes and try to build a better world.

In this context, let us answer the all-important question, "Liberty and morality: can we have both?" The answer is, absolutely yes! Not only can we have both, but we must have both, or eventually we will have neither. As Sir James Russell Lowell said, "The ultimate result of protecting fools from their folly is to fill the planet full of fools."

Our motto should be, "We teach them correct principles, and they govern themselves."

Freedom without responsibility only leads to the destruction of civilization, as evidenced by Rome and other great civilizations of the past. As Alexis de Tocqueville said, "Despotism may govern without faith, but liberty cannot." In a similar vein, Henry Ward Beecher added, "There is no liberty to men who know not how to govern themselves." And Edmund Burke wrote, "What is liberty without wisdom and without virtue?"

Today's political leaders demonstrate their low opinion of the public with every social law they pass. They believe that, if given the right to choose, the citizenry will probably make the wrong choice. Legislators do not think any more in terms of persuading people; they feel the need to force their agenda on the public at the point of a bayonet and the barrel of a gun, in the name of the IRS, the SEC, the FDA, the DEA, the EPA, or a multitude of other ABCs of government authority.

A Challenge to All Lovers of Liberty

My challenge to all lovers of liberty today is to take the moral high ground. Our cause is much more compelling when we can say that we support drug legalization, but do not use mind-altering drugs. That we tolerate legal abortion, but choose not to abort our own future generations. That we support the right to bear arms, but do not misuse handguns. That we favor the right of individuals to meet privately as they please, but do not ourselves discriminate.

In the true spirit of liberty, Voltaire once said, "I disapprove of what you say, but I will defend to the death your right to say it." If we are to be effective in convincing others of the benefits of a tolerant world, we must take the moral high ground by saying, "We may disapprove of what you do, but we will defend to the death your right to do it."

In short, my vision of a responsible free society is one in which we discourage evil, but do not prohibit it. We make our children and students aware of the consequences of drug abuse and other forms of irresponsible behavior. But after all our persuading, if they still want to use harmful drugs, that is their privilege. In a free society, individuals must have the right to do right or wrong, as long as they don't threaten or infringe upon the rights or property of others. They must also suffer the consequences of their actions, as it is from consequences that they learn to choose properly.

We may discourage prostitution or pornography by restricting it to certain areas and to certain ages, but we will not jail or fine those who choose to participate in it privately. If an adult bookstore opens in our neighborhood, we don't run to the law and pass an ordinance, we picket the store and discourage customers. If our religion asks us not to shop on Sunday, we don't pass Sunday "blue" laws forcing stores to close, we simply don't patronize them on Sunday. If we don't like excessive violence and gratuitous sex on TV, we don't write the Federal Communications Commission, we join boycotts of the advertiser's products. Several years ago the owners of Seven Eleven stores removed pornographic magazines from their stores, not because the law required it, but because a group of concerned citizens persuaded them. These actions reflect the true spirit of liberty.

Lovers of liberty should also be strong supporters of the institutions of persuasion, such as churches, charities, foundations, private schools and colleges, and private enterprise. They should engage in many causes of their own free will and choice. They should not rely on the institutions of force, such as government agencies, to carry out the cause of education and the works of charity and welfare. It is not enough simply to pay your taxes and cast your vote and think you've done your part.

It is the duty of every advocate of human liberty to convince the world that we must solve our problems through persuasion and not coercion. Whether the issue is domestic policy or foreign policy, we must recognize that passing another regulation or going to war is not necessarily the only solution to our problems. Simply to pass laws prohibiting the outward symptoms of problems is to sweep the real problems under the rug. It may hide the dirt for a while, but it doesn't dispose of the dirt properly or permanently.

Liberty Under Law

This approach does not mean that laws would not exist. People should have the freedom to act according to their desires, but only to the extent that they do not trample on the rights of others. Rules and regulations, such as traffic laws, need to be established and enforced by private and public institutions in order for a free society to exist. There should be stringent laws against fraud, theft, murder, pollution, and the breaking of contracts, and those laws should be effectively enforced according to the classic principle that the punishment should fit the crime. The full weight of the law should be used to fine and imprison the perpetrators, to compensate the victims, and to safe-guard the rights of the innocent. Yet within this legal framework, we should permit the maximum degree of freedom in allowing people to choose what they think, act and do to themselves without harming others.

Convincing the public of our message, that "persuasion instead of force is the sign of a civilized society," will require a lot of hard work, but it can be rewarding. The key is to make a convincing case for freedom, to present the facts to the public so that they can see the logic of our arguments, and to develop a dialogue with those who may be opposed to our position. Our emphasis must be on educating and persuading, not on arguing and name-calling. For we shall never change our political leaders until we change the people who elect them.

A Vision of an Ideal Society

Martin Luther King, Jr., gave a famous sermon at the Lincoln Memorial in the mid-1960s. In it, King said that he had a dream about the promised land. Well, I too have a vision of an ideal society.

I have a vision of world peace, not because the military have been called in to maintain order, but because we have peace from within and friendship with every nation.

I have a vision of universal prosperity and an end to poverty, not because of foreign aid or government-subsidized welfare, but because each of us has productive, useful employment where every trade is honest and beneficial to both buyer and seller, and where we eagerly help the less fortunate of our own free will.

I have a vision of an inflation-free nation, not because of wage and price controls, but because our nation has an honest money system.

I have a vision of a crime-free society, not because there's a policeman on every corner, but because we respect the rights and property of others.

I have a vision of a drug-free America, not because harmful drugs are illegal, but because we desire to live long, healthy, self-sustaining lives.

I have a vision of an abortion-free society, not because abortion is illegal, but because we firmly believe in the sanctity of life, sexual responsibility, and family values.

I have a vision of a pollution-free and environmentally-sound world, not because of costly controls and arbitrary regulations, but because private enterprise honors its stewardship and commitment to developing rather than exploiting the earth's resources.

I have a vision of a free society, not because of a benevolent dictator commands it, but because we love freedom and the responsibility that goes with it.

The following words, taken from an old Protestant hymn whose author is fittingly anonymous, express the aspiration of every man and every woman in a free society.

Know this, that every soul is free,
To choose his life and what he'll be;
For this eternal truth is given,
That God will force no man to heaven.

He'll call, persuade, direct aright,
And bless with wisdom, love, and light,
In nameless ways be good and kind,
But never force the human mind.

2
Coercivists and Voluntarists
by Donald J. Boudreaux

Categorizing a political position according to some simple left-right scale of values leaves something to be desired. Political views cover such a wide variety of issues that it is impossible to describe adequately any one person merely by identifying where he sits on a lone horizontal line.

Use of the single left-right scale makes impossible a satisfactory description of libertarian (and classical-liberal) attitudes toward government. Libertarians oppose not only government direction of economic affairs, but also government meddling in the personal lives of peaceful people. Does this opposition make libertarians "rightists" (because they promote free enterprise) or "leftists" (because they oppose government meddling in people's private affairs)? As a communications tool, the left-right distinction suffers acute anemia.

Nevertheless, despite widespread dissatisfaction with the familiar left-right – "liberal-conservative" – lingo, such use continues. One reason for its durability is convenience. Never mind that all-important nuances are ignored when describing someone as being, say, "to the right of Richard

Nixon" or "to the left of Lyndon Johnson." The description takes only seconds and doesn't tax the attention of nightly news audiences.

Therefore, no practical good is done by lamenting the mass media's insistence on using a one-dimensional tool for describing political views.

A better strategy for helping to improve political discussion is to devise a set of more descriptive terms.

There is much to be said for a suggestion offered by Professor Richard Gamble, who teaches history at Palm Beach Atlantic University. Gamble proposes that instead of describing someone as either "left" or "right," or "liberal" or "conservative," we describe him as being either a *centralist* or a *decentralist*. This "centralist-decentralist" language would be a vast improvement over the muddled "left-right" language.

Unfortunately, "centralist-decentralist" language contains its own potential confusion—namely, "decentralist" might be taken to mean someone who is indifferent to what Clint Bolick calls "grassroots tyranny." Is there an even better set of labels for a one-dimensional political spectrum? I think so: "coercivist-voluntarist."

At one end of this spectrum are coercivists. Coercivists believe that all order in society must be consciously designed and implemented by a sovereign government power. Coercivists cannot fathom how individuals without mandates from above can ever pattern their actions in a way that is not only orderly, but also peaceful and productive. For the coercivist, direction by sovereign government is as necessary for the creation of social order as the meticulous craftsmanship of a watchmaker is necessary for the creation of a watch.

At the other end of the spectrum are voluntarists. Voluntarists understand two important facts about society that coercivists miss. First, voluntarists understand that social order is inevitable without coercive direction from the state *as long as* the basic rules of private property and voluntary contracting are respected. This inevitability of social order when such rules are observed is the great lesson taught by Adam Smith, Ludwig von Mises, F.A. Hayek, and all of the truly great economists through the ages.

Second, voluntarists understand that coercive social engineering by government – far from promoting social harmony – is fated to *ruin* existing social order. Voluntarists grasp the truth that genuine and productive social order is possible only when each person is free to pursue his own goals in his own way, constrained by no *political* power. Coercive political power is the enemy of social order because it is unavoidably arbitrary – bestowing favors for reasons wholly unrelated to the values the recipients provide to their fellow human beings. And even if by some miracle the exercise of political power could be shorn of its arbitrariness, it can never escape being an exercise conducted in gross ignorance. It is a simpleton's fantasy to imagine that all the immense and detailed knowledge necessary for the successful central direction of human affairs can ever be possessed by government.

Society emerges from the cooperation of hundreds of millions of people, each acting on the basis of his own unique knowledge of individual wants, talents, occupations, and circumstances. No bureaucrat can know enough about software design to outperform Bill Gates, or enough about retailing to successfully second-guess the folks at Walmart, or enough about any of the millions of different industries to outdo people who are highly specialized in their various trades.

The coercivist-voluntarist vocabulary is superior to the left-right, or liberal-conservative, vocabulary at distinguishing liberty's friends from its foes. Support for high taxes and intrusive government commercial regulation is a "liberal" trait. A supporter of high taxes and regulation is also, however, properly labeled a coercivist. But note: no less of a coercivist is the conservative who applauds government regulation of what adults voluntarily read, view, or ingest. Both parties believe that social order will deteriorate into chaos unless government coercion overrides the myriad private choices made by individuals.

Voluntarists are typically accused of endorsing complete freedom of each individual from all restraints. This accusation is nonsense. While they oppose heavy reliance upon *coercively* imposed restraints, sensible voluntarists do not oppose restraints *per se*. Voluntarists, in contrast to coercivists, recognize that superior restraints on individual behavior emerge decentrally and peaceably. Parents restrain their children. Neighbors use both formal and informal means to restrain each other from un-neighborly behaviors. The ability of buyers to choose where to spend their money restrains businesses from abusing customers.

A free society is chock-full of such decentrally and noncoercively imposed restraints. Indeed, it is the voluntary origins of such restraints that make them more trustworthy than coercively imposed restraints. A voluntary restraint grows decentrally from the give and take of everyday life and is sensitive to all the costs and benefits of both the restraint itself and of the restrained behavior. But a coercive restraint too often is the product not of that give and take of all affected parties but, instead, of political deals. And political deals are notoriously biased toward the wishes of the politically well-organized while ignoring the wishes of those unable to form effective political coalitions. What's more, members of the political class often free themselves from the very restraints they foist upon others. Coercively imposed restraints are not social restraints at all; rather, they are arbitrary commands issued by the politically privileged.

The true voluntarist fears nothing as much as he fears coercive power – whether exercised by those on the "left" or the "right."

3
Fundamentals of Voluntaryism
by Carl Watner

Voluntaryism is the doctrine that relations among people should be by mutual consent, or not at all. It represents a means, an end, and an insight. Voluntaryism does not argue for the specific form that voluntary arrangements will take; only that force be abandoned so that individuals in society may flourish. As it is the means which determine the end, the goal of an all voluntary society must be sought voluntarily. People cannot be coerced into freedom. Hence, the use of the free market, education, persuasion, and non-violent resistance are the primary ways to change people's ideas about the State. The voluntaryist insight, that all tyranny and government are grounded upon popular acceptance, explains why voluntary means are sufficient to attain that end.

The Epistemological Argument

Violence is never a means to knowledge. As Isabel Paterson, explained in her book, *The God of the Machine,* "No edict of law can impart to an individual a faculty denied him by nature. A government order cannot mend a broken leg, but it can command the mutilation of a sound body. It cannot bestow intelligence, but it can forbid the use of intelligence." Or, as Baldy Harper used to put it, "You cannot shoot a truth!" The advocate of any form of invasive violence is in a logically precarious situation. Coercion does not convince, nor is it any kind of argument. William Godwin pointed out that force "is contrary to the nature of the intellect, which cannot but be improved by conviction and persuasion," and "if he who employs coercion against me could mold me to his purposes by argument, no doubt, he would... He pretends to punish me because his argument is strong; but he really punishes me because he is weak." Violence contains none of the energies that enhance a civilized human society. At best, it is only capable of expanding the material existence of a few individuals, while narrowing the opportunities of most others.

The Economic Argument

People engage in voluntary exchanges because they anticipate improving their lot; the only individuals capable of judging the merits of an exchange are the parties to it. Voluntaryism follows naturally if no one does anything to stop it. The interplay of natural property and exchanges results in a free market price system, which conveys the necessary information needed to make intelligent economic decisions. Interventionism and collectivism make economic calculation impossible because they disrupt the free market price system. Even the smallest government intervention leads to problems which justify the call for more and more intervention. Also, "controlled" economies leave no room for new inventions, new ways of doing things, or for the "unforeseeable and unpredictable." Free market competition is a learning process which brings about results which no one can know in advance. There is no way to tell how much harm has been done and will continue to be done by political restrictions.

The Moral Argument

The voluntary principle assures us that while we may have the possibility of choosing the worst, we also have the possibility of choosing the best. It provides us the opportunity to make things better, though it doesn't guarantee results. While it dictates that we do not force our idea of "better" on someone else, it protects us from having someone else's idea of "better" imposed on us by force. The use of coercion to compel virtue eliminates its possibility, for to be moral, an act must be uncoerced. If a person is compelled to act in a certain way (or threatened with government sanctions), there is nothing virtuous about his or her behavior. Freedom of choice is a necessary ingredient for the achievement of virtue. Whenever there is a chance for the good life, the risk of a bad one must also be accepted.

The Natural Law Argument

Common sense and reason tell us that nothing can be right by legislative enactment if it is not already right by nature. Epictetus, the Stoic, urged men to defy tyrants in such a way as to cast doubt on the necessity of government itself. "If the government directed them to do something that their reason opposed, they were to defy the government. If it told them to do what their reason would have told them to do anyway, they did not need a government." Just as we do not require a State to dictate what is right or wrong in growing food, manufacturing textiles, or in steel-making, we do not need a government to dictate standards and procedures in any field of endeavor. "In spite of the legislature, the snow will fall when the sun is in Capricorn, and the flowers will bloom when it is in Cancer."

The Means-End Argument

Although certain services and goods are necessary to our survival, it is not essential that they be provided by the government. Voluntaryists oppose the State because it uses coercive means. The means are the seeds which bud into a flower and come into fruition. It is impossible to plant the seed of coercion and then reap the flower of voluntaryism. The coercionist always proposes to compel people to do something, usually by passing laws or electing politicians to office. These laws and officials depend upon physical violence to enforce their wills. Voluntary means, such as non-violent resistance, for example, violate no one's rights. They only serve to nullify laws and politicians by ignoring them. Voluntaryism does not require of people that they violently overthrow their government, or use the electoral process to change it; merely that they shall cease to support their government, whereupon it will fall of its own dead weight. If one takes care of the means, the end will take care of itself.

The Consistency Argument

It is a commonplace observation that the means one uses must be consistent with the goal one seeks. It is impossible to "wage a war for peace" or "fight politics by becoming political." Freedom and private property are total, indivisible concepts that are compromised wherever and whenever the State exists. Since all things are related to one another in our complicated social world, if one man's freedom or private property may be violated (regardless of the justification), then every man's freedom and property are insecure. The superior man can only be sure of his freedom if the inferior man is secure in his rights. We often forget that we can secure our liberty only by preserving it for the most despicable and obnoxious among us, lest we set precedents that can reach us.

The Integrity, Self-Control, and Corruption Argument

It is a fact of human nature that the only person who can think with your brain is you. Neither can a person be compelled to do anything against his or her will, for each person is ultimately responsible for his or her own actions. Governments try to terrorize individuals into submitting to tyranny by grabbing their bodies as hostages and trying to destroy their spirits. This strategy is not successful against the person who harbors the Stoic attitude toward life, and who refuses to allow pain to disturb the equanimity of his or her mind, and the exercise of reason. A government might destroy one's body or property, but it cannot injure one's philosophy of life. Furthermore, the voluntaryist rejects the use of political power because it can only be exercised by implicitly endorsing or using violence to accomplish one's ends. The power to do good to others is also the power to do them harm. Power to compel people, to control other people's lives, is what political power is all about. It violates all the basic principles of voluntaryism: might does not make right; the end never justifies the means; nor may one person coercively interfere in the life of another. Even the smallest amount of political power is dangerous. First, it reduces the capacity of at least some people to lead their own lives in their own way. Second, and more important from the voluntaryist point of view, is what it does to the person wielding the power: it corrupts that person's character.

4
The Anatomy of the State
by Murray N. Rothbard

What the State Is Not

The State is almost universally considered an institution of social service. Some theorists venerate the State as the apotheosis of society; others regard it as an amiable, though often inefficient, organization for achieving social ends; but almost all regard it as a necessary means for achieving the goals of mankind, a means to be ranged against the "private sector" and often winning in this competition of resources. With the rise of democracy, the identification of the State with society has been redoubled, until it is common to hear sentiments expressed which violate virtually every tenet of reason and common sense such as, "we are the government." The useful collective term "we" has enabled an ideological camouflage to be thrown over the reality of political life. If "we are the government," then anything a government does to an individual is not only just and untyrannical but also "voluntary" on the part of the individual concerned. If the government has incurred a huge public debt which must be paid by taxing one group for the benefit of another, this reality of burden is obscured by saying that "we owe it to ourselves"; if the government conscripts a man, or throws him into jail for dissident opinion, then he is "doing it to himself" and, therefore, nothing untoward has occurred. Under this reasoning, any Jews murdered by the Nazi government were *not* murdered; instead, they must have "committed suicide," since they *were* the government (which was democratically chosen), and, therefore, anything the government did to them was voluntary on their part. One would not think it necessary to belabor this point, and yet the overwhelming bulk of the people hold this fallacy to a greater or lesser degree.

We must, therefore, emphasize that "we" are *not* the government; the government is *not* "us." The government does not in any accurate sense "represent" the majority of the people.* But, even if it did, even if 70 percent of the people decided to murder the remaining 30 percent, this would still be murder and would not be voluntary suicide on the part of the slaughtered minority.* No organicist metaphor, no irrelevant bromide that "we are all part of one another," must be permitted to obscure this basic fact.

If, then, the State is not "us," if it is not "the human family" getting together to decide mutual problems, if it is not a lodge meeting or country club, what is it? Briefly, the State is that organization in society which attempts to maintain a monopoly of the use of force and violence in a given territorial area; in particular, it is the only organization in society that obtains its revenue not by voluntary contribution or payment for services rendered, but by coercion. While other individuals or institutions obtain their income by production of goods and services and by the peaceful and voluntary sale of these goods and services to others, the State obtains its revenue by the use of compulsion; that is, by the use and the threat of the jailhouse and the bayonet.* Having used force and violence to obtain its revenue, the State generally goes on to regulate and dictate the other actions of its individual subjects. One would think that simple observation of all States through history and over the globe would be proof enough of this assertion;

---

*For citations, see: http://goo.gl/Q4NA6

but the miasma of myth has lain so long over State activity that elaboration is necessary.

What the State Is

Man is born naked into the world, and needing to use his mind to learn how to take the resources given him by nature, and to transform them (for example, by investment in "capital") into shapes and forms and places where the resources can be used for the satisfaction of his wants and the advancement of his standard of living. The only way by which man can do this is by the use of his mind and energy to transform resources ("production") and to exchange these products for products created by others. Man has found that, through the process of voluntary, mutual exchange, the productivity and hence the living standards of all participants in exchange may increase enormously. The only "natural" course for man to survive and to attain wealth, therefore, is by using his mind and energy to engage in the production-and-exchange process. He does this, first, by finding natural resources, and then by transforming them (by "mixing his labor" with them, as Locke puts it), to make them his individual *property*, and then by exchanging this property for the similarly obtained property of others. The social path dictated by the requirements of man's nature, therefore, is the path of "property rights" and the "free market" of gift or exchange of such rights. Through this path, men have learned how to avoid the "jungle" methods of fighting over scarce resources so that A can only acquire them at the expense of B and, instead, to multiply those resources enormously in peaceful and harmonious production and exchange.

The great German sociologist Franz Oppenheimer pointed out that there are two mutually exclusive ways of acquiring wealth; one, the above way of production and exchange, he called the "economic means." The other way is simpler in that it does not require productivity; it is the way of seizure of another's goods or services by the use of force and violence. This is the method of one-sided confiscation, of theft of the property of others. This is the method which Oppenheimer termed "the political means" to wealth. It should be clear that the peaceful use of reason and energy in production is the "natural" path for man: the means for his survival and prosperity on this earth. It should be equally clear that the coercive, exploitative means is contrary to natural law; it is parasitic, for instead of adding to production, it subtracts from it. The "political means" siphons production off to a parasitic and destructive individual or group; and this siphoning not only subtracts from the number producing, but also lowers the producer's incentive to produce beyond his own subsistence. In the long run, the robber destroys his own subsistence by dwindling or eliminating the source of his own supply. But not only that; even in the short run, the predator is acting contrary to his own true nature as a man.

We are now in a position to answer more fully the question: what is the *State*? The State, in the words of Oppenheimer, is the "organization of the political means"; it is the systematization of the predatory process over a given territory.* For crime, at best, is sporadic and uncertain; the parasitism is ephemeral, and the coercive, parasitic lifeline may be cut off at any time by the resistance of the victims. The State provides a legal, orderly, systematic channel for the predation of private property; it renders certain, secure, and relatively "peaceful" the lifeline of the parasitic caste in society.* Since production must always precede predation, the free market is anterior to the State. The State has never been created by a "social contract"; it has always been born in conquest and exploitation. The classic paradigm was a conquering tribe pausing in its time-honored method of looting and murdering a conquered tribe, to realize that the time-span of plunder would be longer and more secure, and the situation more pleasant, if the conquered tribe were allowed to live and produce, with the conquerors settling among them as rulers exacting a steady annual tribute.* One method of the birth of a State may be illustrated as follows: in the hills of southern "Ruritania," a bandit group manages to obtain physical control over the territory, and finally the bandit chieftain proclaims himself "King of the sovereign and independent government of South Ruritania"; and, if he and his men have the force to maintain this rule for a while, lo and behold!, a new State has joined the "family of nations," and the former bandit leaders have been transformed into the lawful nobility of the realm.

How the State Preserves Itself

Once a State has been established, the problem of the ruling group or "caste" is how to maintain their rule.* While force is their *modus operandi*, their basic and long-run problem is ideological. For in order to continue in office, *any* government (not simply a "democratic" government) must have the support of the majority of its subjects. This support, it must be noted, need not be active enthusiasm; it may well be passive resignation as if to an inevitable law of nature. But support in the sense of acceptance of some sort it must be; else the minority of State rulers would eventually be outweighed by the active resistance of the majority of the public. Since predation must be supported out of the surplus of production, it is necessarily true that the class constituting the State – the full-time bureaucracy (and nobility) – must be a rather small minority in the land, although it may, of course, purchase allies among important groups in the population. Therefore, the chief task of the rulers is always to secure the active or resigned acceptance of the majority of the citizens.*

Of course, one method of securing support is through the creation of vested economic interests. Therefore, the King alone cannot rule; he must have a sizable group of followers who enjoy the prerequisites of rule, for example, the members of the State apparatus, such as the full-time bureaucracy or the established nobility.* But this still secures only a minority of eager supporters, and even the essential purchasing of support by subsidies and other grants of privilege still does not obtain the consent of the majority. For this essential acceptance, the majority must be persuaded by *ideology* that their government is good, wise and, at least, inevitable, and certainly better than other conceivable alternatives. Promoting this ideology among the people is the vital social task of the "intellectuals." For the masses of men do not create their own ideas, or indeed think through these ideas independently; they follow passively the ideas adopted and disseminated by the body of intellectuals. The intellectuals are, therefore, the "opinion-molders" in society. And since it is precisely a molding of opinion that the State most desperately needs, the basis for age-old alliance between the State and the intellectuals becomes clear.

It is evident that the State needs the intellectuals; it is not so evident why intellectuals need the State. Put simply, we may state that the intellectual's livelihood in the free market is never too secure; for the intellectual must depend on the values and choices of the masses of his fellow men, and it is precisely characteristic of the masses that they are generally uninterested in intellectual matters. The State, on the other hand, is willing to offer the intellectuals a secure and permanent berth in the State apparatus; and thus a secure income and the panoply of prestige. For the intellectuals will be handsomely rewarded for the important function they perform for the State rulers, of which group they now become a part.*

The alliance between the State and the intellectuals was symbolized in the eager desire of professors at the University of Berlin in the nineteenth century to form the "intellectual bodyguard of the House of Hohenzollern." In the present day, let us note the revealing comment of an eminent Marxist scholar concerning Professor Wittfogel's critical study of ancient Oriental despotism: "The civilization which Professor Wittfogel is so bitterly attacking was one which could make poets and scholars into officials."* Of innumerable examples, we may cite the recent development of the "science" of strategy, in the service of the government's main violence-wielding arm, the military.* A venerable institution, furthermore, is the official or "court" historian, dedicated to purveying the rulers' views of their own and their predecessors' actions.*

Many and varied have been the arguments by which the State and its intellectuals have induced their subjects to support their rule. Basically, the strands of argument may be summed up as follows: (a) the State rulers are great and wise men (they "rule by divine right," they are the "aristocracy" of men, they are the "scientific experts"), much greater and wiser than the good but rather simple subjects, and (b) rule by the extent government is inevitable, absolutely necessary, and far better, than the indescribable evils that would ensue upon its downfall. The union of Church and State was one of the oldest and most successful of these ideological devices. The ruler was either anointed by God or, in the case of the absolute rule of many Oriental despotisms, was himself God; hence, any resistance to his rule would be blasphemy. The States' priestcraft performed the basic intellectual function of obtaining popular support and even worship for the rulers.*

Another successful device was to instill fear of any alternative systems of rule or nonrule. The present rulers, it was maintained, supplied the citizens an essential service for which they should be most grateful: protection against sporadic criminals and marauders. For the State, to preserve its own monopoly of predation, did indeed see to it that private and unsystematic crime was kept to a minimum; the State has always been jealous of its own preserve. Especially has the State been successful in recent centuries in instilling fear of *other* State rulers. Since the land area of the globe has been parceled out among particular States, one of the basic doctrines of the State was to identify itself with the territory it governed. Since most men tend to love their homeland, the identification of that land and its people with the State was a means of making natural patriotism work to the State's advantage. If "Ruritania" was being attacked by "Walldavia," the first task of the State and its intellectuals was to convince the people of Ruritania that the attack was really upon *them* and not simply upon the ruling caste. In this way, a war between *rulers* was converted into a war between *peoples*, with each people coming to the defense of its rulers in the erroneous belief that the rulers were defending *them*. This device of "nationalism" has only been successful, in Western civilization, in recent centuries; it was not too long ago that the mass of subjects regarded wars as irrelevant battles between various sets of nobles.

Many and subtle are the ideological weapons that the State has wielded through the centuries. One excellent weapon has been tradition. The longer that the rule of a State has been able to preserve itself, the more powerful this weapon; for then, the X Dynasty or the Y State has the seeming weight of centuries of tradition behind it.* Worship of one's ancestors, then, becomes a none too subtle means of worship of one's ancient rulers. The greatest danger to the State is independent intellectual criticism; there is no better way to stifle that criticism than to attack any isolated voice, any raiser of new doubts, as a profane violator of the wisdom of his ancestors.

Another potent ideological force is to deprecate the *individual* and exalt the collectivity of society. For since any given rule implies majority acceptance, any ideological danger to that rule can only start from one or a few independently-thinking individuals. The new idea, much less the new *critical* idea, must needs begin as a small minority opinion; therefore, the State must nip the view in the bud by ridiculing any view that defies the opinions of the mass. "Listen only to your brothers" or "adjust to society" thus become ideological weapons for crushing individual dissent.* By such measures, the masses will never learn of the nonexistence of their Emperor's clothes.*

It is also important for the State to make its rule seem inevitable; even if its reign is disliked, it will then be met with passive resignation, as witness the familiar coupling of "death and taxes." One method is to induce historiographical determinism, as opposed to individual freedom of will. If the X Dynasty rules us, this is because the Inexorable Laws of History (or the Divine Will, or the Absolute, or the Material Productive Forces) have so decreed and nothing any puny individuals may do can change this inevitable decree.

It is also important for the State to inculcate in its subjects an aversion to any "conspiracy theory of history"; for a search for "conspiracies" means a search for motives and an attribution of responsibility for historical misdeeds. If, however, any tyranny imposed by the State, or venality, or aggressive war, was caused *not* by the State rulers but by mysterious and arcane "social forces," or by the imperfect state of the world or, if in some way, *everyone* was responsible ("We Are All Murderers," proclaims one slogan), then there is no point to the people becoming indignant or rising up against such misdeeds. Furthermore, an attack on "conspiracy theories" means that the subjects will become more gullible in believing the "general welfare" reasons that are always put forth by the State for engaging in any of its despotic actions. A "conspiracy theory" can unsettle the system by causing the public to doubt the State's ideological propaganda.

Another tried and true method for bending subjects to the State's will is inducing guilt. Any increase in private well-being can be attacked as "unconscionable greed," "materialism," or "excessive affluence," profit-making can be attacked as "exploitation" and "usury," mutually beneficial exchanges denounced as "selfishness," and somehow with the conclusion always being drawn that more resources should be siphoned from the private to the "public sector." The induced guilt makes the public more ready to do just that. For while individual persons tend to indulge in "selfish greed," the failure of the State's rulers to engage in exchanges is supposed to signify *their* devotion to higher and nobler causes – parasitic predation being apparently morally and esthetically lofty as compared to peaceful and productive work.

In the present more secular age, the divine right of the State has been supplemented by the invocation of a new god, Science. State rule is now proclaimed as being ultrascientific, as constituting planning by experts. But while "reason" is invoked more than in previous centuries, this is not the true reason of the individual and his exercise of free will; it is still collectivist and determinist, still implying holistic aggregates and coercive manipulation of passive subjects by their rulers.

The increasing use of scientific jargon has permitted the State's intellectuals to weave obscurantist apologia for State rule that would have only met with derision by the populace of a simpler age. A robber who justified his theft by saying that he really helped his victims, by his spending giving a boost to retail trade, would find few converts; but when this theory is clothed in Keynesian equations and impressive references to the "multiplier effect," it unfortunately carries more conviction. And so the assault on common sense proceeds, each age performing the task in its own ways.

Thus, ideological support being vital to the State, it must unceasingly try to impress the public with its "legitimacy," to distinguish its activities from those of mere brigands. The unremitting determination of its assaults on common sense is no accident, for as Mencken vividly maintained:

> "The average man, whatever his errors otherwise, at least sees clearly that government is something lying outside him and outside the generality of his fellow men – that it is a separate, independent, and hostile power, only partly under his control, and capable of doing him great harm. Is it a fact of no significance that robbing the government is everywhere regarded as a crime of less magnitude than robbing an individual, or even a corporation?... What lies behind all this, I believe, is a deep sense of the fundamental antagonism between the government and the people it governs. It is apprehended, not as a committee of citizens chosen to carry on the communal business of the whole population, but as a separate and autonomous corporation, mainly devoted to exploiting the population for the benefit of its own members... When a private citizen is robbed, a worthy man is deprived of the fruits of his industry and thrift; when the government is robbed, the worst that happens is that certain rogues and loafers have less money to play with than they had before. The notion that they have earned that money is never entertained; to most sensible men it would seem ludicrous."*

How the State Transcends Its Limits

As Bertrand de Jouvenel has sagely pointed out, through the centuries men have formed concepts designed to check and limit the exercise of State rule; and, one after another, the State, using its intellectual allies, has been able to transform these concepts into intellectual rubber stamps of legitimacy and virtue to attach to its decrees and actions. Originally, in Western Europe, the concept of divine sovereignty held that the kings may rule only according to divine law; the kings turned the concept into a rubber stamp of divine approval for any of the kings' actions. The concept of parliamentary democracy began as a popular check upon absolute monarchical rule; it ended with parliament being the essential part of the State and its every act totally sovereign. As de Jouvenel concludes:

"Many writers on theories of sovereignty have worked out one... of these restrictive devices. But in the end every single such theory has, sooner or later, lost its original purpose, and come to act merely as a springboard to Power, by providing it with the powerful aid of an invisible sovereign with whom it could in time successfully identify itself."*

Similarly with more specific doctrines: the "natural rights" of the individual enshrined in John Locke and the Bill of Rights, became a statist "right to a job"; utilitarianism turned from arguments for liberty to arguments against resisting the State's invasions of liberty, etc.

Certainly the most ambitious attempt to impose limits on the State has been the Bill of Rights and other restrictive parts of the American Constitution, in which written limits on government became the fundamental law to be interpreted by a judiciary supposedly independent of the other branches of government. All Americans are familiar with the process by which the construction of limits in the Constitution has been inexorably broadened over the last century. But few have been as keen as Professor Charles Black to see that the State has, in the process, largely transformed judicial review itself from a limiting device to yet another instrument for furnishing ideological legitimacy to the government's actions. For if a judicial decree of "unconstitutional" is a mighty check to government power, an implicit or explicit verdict of "constitutional" is a mighty weapon for fostering public acceptance of ever-greater government power.

Professor Black begins his analysis by pointing out the crucial necessity of "legitimacy" for any government to endure, this legitimation signifying basic majority acceptance of the government and its actions.* Acceptance of legitimacy becomes a particular problem in a country such as the United States, where "substantive limitations are built into the theory on which the government rests." What is needed, adds Black, is a means by which the government can assure the public that its increasing powers are, indeed, "constitutional." And this, he concludes, has been the major historic function of judicial review.

Let Black illustrate the problem:

"The supreme risk [to the government] is that of disaffection and a feeling of outrage widely disseminated throughout the population, and loss of moral authority by the government as such, however long it may be propped up by force or inertia or the lack of an appealing and immediately available alternative. Almost everybody living under a government of limited powers, must sooner or later be subjected to some governmental action which as a matter of private opinion he regards as outside the power of government or positively forbidden to government. A man is drafted, though he finds nothing in the Constitution about being drafted... A farmer is told how much wheat he can raise; he believes, and he discovers that some respectable lawyers believe with him, that the government has no more right to tell him how much wheat he can grow than it has to tell his daughter whom she can marry. A man goes to the federal penitentiary for saying what he wants to, and he paces his cell reciting... "Congress shall make no laws abridging the freedom of speech."... A businessman is told what he can ask, and must ask, for buttermilk.

"The danger is real enough that each of these people (and who is not of their number?) will confront the concept of governmental limitation with the reality (as he sees it) of the flagrant overstepping of actual limits, and draw the obvious conclusion as to the status of his government with respect to legitimacy."*

This danger is averted by the State's propounding the doctrine that one agency must have the ultimate decision on constitutionality and that this agency, in the last analysis, must be *part of* the federal government.* For while the seeming independence of the federal judiciary has played a vital part in making its actions virtual Holy Writ for the bulk of the people, it is also and ever true that the judiciary is part and parcel of the government apparatus and appointed by the executive and legislative branches. Black admits that this means that the State has set itself up as a judge in its own cause, thus violating a basic juridical principle for aiming at just decisions. He brusquely denies the possibility of any alternative.*

Black adds:

"The problem, then, is to devise such governmental means of deciding as will [hopefully] reduce to a tolerable minimum the intensity of the objection that government is judge in its own cause. Having done this, you can only hope that this objection, *though theoretically still tenable* [italics mine], will practically lose enough of its force that the legitimating work of the deciding institution can win acceptance."*

In the last analysis, Black finds the achievement of justice and legitimacy from the State's perpetual judging of its own cause as "something of a miracle."*

Applying his thesis to the famous conflict between the Supreme Court and the New Deal, Professor Black keenly chides his fellow pro-New Deal colleagues for their shortsightedness in denouncing judicial obstruction:

"[t]he standard version of the story of the New Deal and the Court, though accurate in its way, displaces the emphasis... It concentrates on the difficulties; it almost forgets how the whole thing turned out. The upshot of the matter was [and this is what I like to emphasize] that after some twenty-four months of balking... the Supreme Court, without a single change in the law of its composition, or, indeed, in its actual manning, *placed the affirmative stamp of legitimacy on the New Deal, and on the whole new conception of government in America.*"*

In this way, the Supreme Court was able to put the quietus on the large body of Americans who had had strong constitutional objections to the New Deal:

"Of course, not everyone was satisfied. The Bonnie Prince Charlie of constitutionally commanded *laissez faire* still stirs the hearts of a few zealots in the Highlands of choleric unreality. But there is no longer any significant or dangerous public doubt as to the constitutional power of Congress to deal as it does with the national economy...

"We had no means, other than the Supreme Court, for imparting legitimacy to the New Deal."*

As Black recognizes, one major political theorist who recognized – and largely in advance – the glaring loophole in a constitutional limit on government of placing the ultimate interpreting power in the Supreme Court was John C. Calhoun. Calhoun was not content with the "miracle," but instead proceeded to a profound analysis of the constitutional problem. In his *Disquisition*, Calhoun demonstrated the inherent tendency of the State to break through the limits of such a constitution:

"A written constitution certainly has many and considerable advantages, but it is a great mistake to suppose that the mere insertion of provisions to restrict and limit the power of the government, *without investing those for whose protection they are inserted with the means of enforcing their observance* [my italics] will be sufficient to prevent the major and dominant party from abusing its powers. Being the party in possession of the government, they will, from the same constitution of man which makes government necessary to protect society, be in favor of the powers granted by the constitution and opposed to the restrictions intended to limit them...

"The minor or weaker party, on the contrary, would take the opposite direction and regard them [the restrictions] as essential to their protection against the dominant party... But where there are no means by which they could compel the major party to observe the restrictions, the only resort left them would be a strict construction of the constitution... To this the major party would oppose a liberal construction... It would be construction against construction – the one to contract and the other to enlarge the powers of the government to the utmost. But of what possible avail could the strict construction of the minor party be, against the liberal construction of the major, when the one would have all the power of the government to carry its construction into effect and the other be deprived of all means of enforcing its construction? In a contest so unequal, the result would not be doubtful. The party in favor of the restrictions would be overpowered... The end of the contest would be the subversion of the constitution... the restrictions would ultimately be annulled and the government be converted into one of unlimited powers."*

One of the few political scientists who appreciated Calhoun's analysis of the Constitution was Professor J. Allen Smith. Smith noted that the Constitution was designed with checks and balances to limit any one governmental power and yet had then developed a Supreme Court with the monopoly of ultimate interpreting power. If the Federal Government was created to check invasions of individual liberty by the separate states, who was to check the Federal power? Smith maintained that implicit in the check-and-balance idea of the Constitution was the concomitant view that no one branch of government may be conceded the ultimate power of interpretation: "It was assumed by the people that the new government could not be permitted to determine the limits of its own authority, since this would make it, and not the Constitution, supreme."*

The solution advanced by Calhoun (and seconded, in this century, by such writers as Smith) was, of course, the famous doctrine of the "concurrent majority." If any substantial minority interest in the country, specifically a state government, believed that the Federal Government was exceeding its powers and encroaching on that minority, the minority would have the right to veto this exercise of power as unconstitutional. Applied to state governments, this theory implied the right of "nullification" of a Federal law or ruling within a state's jurisdiction.

In theory, the ensuing constitutional system would assure that the Federal Government check any state invasion of individual rights, while the states would check excessive Federal power over the individual. And yet, while limitations would undoubtedly be more effective than at present, there are many difficulties and problems in the Calhoun solution. If, indeed, a subordinate interest should rightfully have a veto over matters concerning it, then why stop with the states? Why not place veto power in counties, cities, wards? Furthermore, interests are not only sectional, they are also occupational, social, etc. What of bakers or taxi drivers or any other occupation? Should *they* not be permitted a veto power over their own lives? This brings us to the important point that the nullification theory confines its checks to *agencies of government* itself. Let us not forget that federal and state governments, and their respective branches, are still states, are still guided by their own state interests rather than by the interests of the private citizens. What is to prevent the Calhoun system from working in reverse, with states tyrannizing over *their* citizens and only vetoing the federal government when it tries to intervene to *stop* that state tyranny? Or for states to acquiesce in federal tyranny? What is to prevent federal and state governments from forming mutually profitable alliances for the joint exploitation of the citizenry? And even if the private occupational groupings were to be given some form of "functional" representation in government, what is to prevent them from using the State to gain subsidies and other special privileges for themselves or from imposing compulsory cartels on their own members?

In short, Calhoun does not push his pathbreaking theory on concurrence far enough: he does not push it down to the *individual* himself. If the individual, after all, is the one whose rights are to be protected, then a consistent theory of concurrence would imply veto power by every individual; that is, some form of "unanimity principle." When Calhoun wrote that it should be "impossible to put or to keep it [the government] in action without the concurrent consent of all," he was, perhaps unwittingly, implying just such a conclusion.* But such speculation begins to take us away from our subject, for down this path lie political systems which could hardly be called "States" at all.* For one thing, just as the right of nullification for a state logically implies its right of *secession*, so a right of individual nullification would imply the right of any individual to "secede" from the State under which he lives.*

Thus, the State has invariably shown a striking talent for the expansion of its powers beyond any limits that might be imposed upon it. Since the State necessarily lives by the compulsory confiscation of private capital, and since its expansion necessarily involves ever-greater incursions on private individuals and private enterprise, we must assert that the State is profoundly and inherently *anti*-capitalist. In a sense, our position is the reverse of the Marxist dictum that the State is the "executive committee" of the ruling class in the present day, supposedly the capitalists. Instead, the State – the organization of the political means – constitutes, and is the source of, the "ruling class" (rather, ruling *caste*), and is in permanent opposition to *genuinely* private capital. We may, therefore, say with de Jouvenel:

> "Only those who know nothing of any time but their own, who are completely in the dark as to the manner of Power's behaving through thousands of years, would regard these proceedings [nationalization, the income tax, etc.] as the fruit of a particular set of doctrines. They are in fact the normal manifestations of Power, and differ not at all in their nature from Henry VIII's confiscation of the monasteries. The same principle is at work; the hunger for authority, the thirst for resources; and in all of these operations the same characteristics are present, including the rapid elevation of the dividers of the spoils. Whether it is Socialist or whether it is not, Power must always be at war with the capitalist authorities and despoil the capitalists of their accumulated wealth; in doing so it obeys the law of its nature."*

What the State Fears

What the State fears above all, of course, is any fundamental threat to its own power and its own existence. The death of a State can come about in two major ways: (a) through conquest by another State, or (b) through revolutionary overthrow by its own subjects – in short, by war or revolution. War and revolution, as the two basic threats, invariably arouse in the State rulers their maximum efforts and maximum propaganda among the people. As stated above, any way must always be used to mobilize the people to come to the State's defense in the belief that they are defending themselves. The fallacy of the idea becomes evident when conscription is wielded against those who refuse to "defend" themselves and are, therefore, forced into joining the State's military band: needless to add, no "defense" is permitted them against this act of "their own" State.

In war, State power is pushed to its ultimate, and, under the slogans of "defense" and "emergency," it can impose a tyranny upon the public such as might be openly resisted in time of peace. War thus provides many benefits to a State, and indeed every modern war has brought to the warring peoples a permanent legacy of increased State burdens upon society. War, moreover, provides to a State tempting opportunities for conquest of land areas over which it may exercise its monopoly of force. Randolph Bourne was certainly correct when he wrote that "war is the health of the State," but to any particular State a war may spell either health or grave injury.*

We may test the hypothesis that the State is largely interested in protecting *itself* rather than its subjects by asking: which category of crimes does the State pursue and punish most intensely – those against private citizens or those against *itself*? The gravest crimes in the State's lexicon are almost invariably not invasions of private person or property, but dangers to its *own* contentment, for example, treason, desertion of a soldier to the enemy, failure to register for the draft, subversion and subversive conspiracy, assassination of rulers and such economic crimes against the State as counterfeiting its money or evasion of its income tax. Or compare the degree of zeal devoted to pursuing the man who assaults a policeman, with the attention that the State pays to the assault of an ordinary citizen. Yet, curiously, the State's openly assigned priority to its *own* defense against the public strikes few people as inconsistent with its presumed *raison d'être*.*

How States Relate to One Another

Since the territorial area of the earth is divided among different States, inter-State relations must occupy much of a State's time and energy. The natural tendency of a State is to expand its power, and externally such expansion takes place by conquest of a territorial area. Unless a territory is stateless or uninhabited, any such expansion involves an inherent conflict of interest between one set of State rulers and another. Only one set of rulers can obtain a monopoly of coercion over any given territorial area at any one time: complete power over a territory by State X can only be obtained by the expulsion of State Y. War, while risky, will be an ever-present tendency of States, punctuated by periods of peace and by shifting alliances and coalitions between States.

We have seen that the "internal" or "domestic" attempt to limit the State, in the seventeenth through nineteenth centuries, reached its most notable form in constitutionalism. Its "external," or "foreign affairs," counterpart was the development of "international law," especially such forms as the "laws of war" and "neutrals' rights."* Parts of international law were originally purely private, growing out of the need of merchants and traders everywhere to protect their property and adjudicate disputes. Examples are admiralty law and the law merchant. But even the governmental rules emerged voluntarily and were not imposed by any international super-State. The object of the "laws of war" was to limit inter-State destruction *to the State apparatus itself*, thereby preserving the innocent "civilian" public from the slaughter and devastation of war. The object of the development of neutrals' rights was to preserve private civilian international commerce, even with "enemy" countries, from seizure by one of the warring parties. The overriding aim, then, was to limit the extent of any war, and, particularly to limit its destructive impact on the private citizens of the neutral and even the warring countries.

The jurist F.J.P. Veale charmingly describes such "civilized warfare" as it briefly flourished in fifteenth-century Italy:

> "the rich burghers and merchants of medieval Italy were too busy

making money and enjoying life to undertake the hardships and dangers of soldiering themselves. So they adopted the practice of hiring mercenaries to do their fighting for them, and, being thrifty, business-like folk, they dismissed their mercenaries immediately after their services could be dispensed with. Wars were, therefore, fought by armies hired for each campaign... For the first time, soldiering became a reasonable and comparatively harmless profession. The generals of that period maneuvered against each other, often with consummate skill, but when one had won the advantage, his opponent generally either retreated or surrendered. It was a recognized rule that a town could only be sacked if it offered resistance: immunity could always be purchased by paying a ransom... As one natural consequence, no town ever resisted, it being obvious that a government too weak to defend its citizens had forfeited their allegiance. Civilians had little to fear from the dangers of war which were the concern only of professional soldiers."*

The well-nigh absolute separation of the private civilian from the State's wars in eighteenth-century Europe is highlighted by Nef:

"Even postal communications were not successfully restricted for long in wartime. Letters circulated without censorship, with a freedom that astonishes the twentieth-century mind... The subjects of two warring nations talked to each other if they met, and when they could not meet, corresponded, not as enemies but as friends. The modern notion hardly existed that... subjects of any enemy country are partly accountable for the belligerent acts of their rulers. Nor had the warring rulers any firm disposition to stop communications with subjects of the enemy. The old inquisitorial practices of espionage in connection with religious worship and belief were disappearing, and no comparable inquisition in connection with political or economic communications was even contemplated. Passports were originally created to provide safe conduct in time of war. During most of the eighteenth century it seldom occurred to Europeans to abandon their travels in a foreign country which their own was fighting.*

"And trade being increasingly recognized as beneficial to both parties; eighteenth-century warfare also counterbalances a considerable amount of 'trading with the enemy.'"*

How far States have transcended rules of civilized warfare in this century needs no elaboration here. In the modern era of total war, combined with the technology of total destruction, the very idea of keeping war limited to the State apparati seems even more quaint and obsolete than the original Constitution of the United States.

When States are not at war, agreements are often necessary to keep frictions at a minimum. One doctrine that has gained curiously wide acceptance is the alleged "sanctity of treaties." This concept is treated as the counterpart of the "sanctity of contract." But a treaty and a genuine contract have nothing in common. A contract transfers, in a precise manner, titles to private property. Since a government does not, in any proper sense, "own" its territorial area, any agreements that it concludes do not confer titles to property. If, for example, Mr. Jones sells or gives his land to Mr. Smith, Jones's heir cannot legitimately descend upon Smith's heir and claim the land as rightfully his. The property title has already been transferred. Old Jones's contract is automatically binding upon young Jones, because the former had already transferred the property; young Jones, therefore, has no property claim. Young Jones can only claim that which he has inherited from old Jones, and old Jones can only bequeath property which he still owns. But if, at a certain date, the government of, say, Ruritania is coerced or even bribed by the government of Waldavia into giving up some of its territory, it is absurd to claim that the governments or inhabitants of the two countries are forever barred from a claim to reunification of Ruritania on the grounds of the sanctity of a treaty. Neither the people nor the land of northwest Ruritania are owned by either of the two governments. As a corollary, one government can certainly not bind, by the dead hand of the past, a later government through treaty. A revolutionary government which overthrew the king of Ruritania could, similarly, hardly be called to account for the king's actions or debts, for a government is not, as is a child, a true "heir" to its predecessor's property.

History as a Race Between State Power and Social Power

Just as the two basic and mutually exclusive interrelations between men are peaceful cooperation or coercive exploitation, production or predation, so the history of mankind, particularly its economic history, may be considered as a contest between these two principles. On the one hand, there is creative productivity, peaceful exchange and cooperation; on the other, coercive dictation and predation over those social relations. Albert Jay Nock happily termed these contesting forces: "social power" and "State power."* Social power is man's *power over nature*, his cooperative transformation of nature's resources and insight into nature's laws, for the benefit of all participating individuals. Social power is the power over nature, the living standards achieved by men in mutual exchange. State power, as we have seen, is the coercive and parasitic seizure of this production – a draining of the fruits of society for the benefit of non-productive (actually anti-productive) rulers. While social power is over nature, State power is *power over man*. Through history, man's productive and creative forces have, time and again, carved out new ways of transforming nature for man's benefit. These have been the times when social power has spurted ahead of State power, and when the degree of State encroachment over society has considerably lessened. But always, after a greater or smaller time lag, the State has moved into these new areas, to cripple and confiscate social power once more.* If the seventeenth through the nineteenth centuries were, in many countries of the West, times of accelerating social power, and a corollary increase in freedom, peace, and material welfare, the twentieth century has been primarily an age in which State power has been catching up – with a consequent reversion to slavery, war, and destruction.*

In this century, the human race faces, once again, the virulent reign of the State – of the State now armed with the fruits of man's creative powers, confiscated and perverted to its own aims. The last few centuries were times when men tried to place constitutional and other limits on the State, only to find that such limits, as with all other attempts, have failed. Of all the numerous forms that governments have taken over the centuries, of all the concepts and institutions that have been tried, none has succeeded in keeping the State in check. The problem of the State is evidently as far from solution as ever. Perhaps new paths of inquiry must be explored, if the successful, final solution of the State question is ever to be attained.*

5
Thoughts on Nonviolence
by Karl H. Meyer

What is nonviolence? It is a way of life based on these human beliefs: Human conflicts can be resolved without violence or force; organized social aggression can be faced and turned back effectively without war and without killing anybody; most crime problems can be addressed more effectively without the use of violent methods or punishment or restraint; people well-educated in the use of nonviolent methods will almost always be more effective in human relations than those who use physical threats and weapons.

Commitment to nonviolence requires us to find solutions that address the needs and feelings of all parties. Resorting to violence means that one party will lose and be forced to give up when the other party wins. Nonviolence begins with respect for the needs and feelings of others, and a serious attempt to appreciate their point of view. The methods of nonviolence are communication, negotiation, mediation, arbitration and nonviolent forms of protest and resistance, when other forms of communication fail to resolve a conflict. When these methods are used with skill and persistence, most conflicts can be resolved without any party feeling the need to resort to violence. Organized, persistent nonviolent action can overcome oppression and resist aggression more effectively than violent means.

The fact is that all of us use nonviolent methods in most of our human relationships, most of the time. It would be a sorry world if we didn't. What would it be like if we used violence instead of negotiation every time that someone else had something that we wanted? What would it be like if we used violent retaliation every time that someone else did something that obstructed us or angered us? We use nonviolent methods in most of our family disputes. We use it in our schools, our work relationships and our commercial trading transactions. We use it in almost all relationships between communities within the established borders of nations, and in most relations between nations.

Many of us never resort to the explicit use of violence at all. Most others resort to it only in occasional situations.

We carry on most of our activities within a structure of law and customary principles of nonviolent relationship. It may seem that this structure is only held together by the ultimate threat of police force; but, in fact, the fabric of social relationships in families, in groups and in larger communities has always been held together primarily by voluntary assent to common principles of social organization.

Throughout history it has been common to resolve conflicts between nations by warfare and the use of force. Yet even here the majority of relationships have been governed by negotiated agreements, treaties, laws and customs.

Mahatma Gandhi and Martin Luther King Jr. did not invent nonviolence. Their instinctive contribution was to show how organized nonviolent action could solve intractable situations of longstanding oppression and conflict. Before them, others believed that these problems could not be solved, or could be solved only by violent revolt.

Mahatma Gandhi and Dr. King showed how we can take the nonviolent methods that we use most of the time in everyday relationships, and develop them as powerful tools to solve the most difficult problems of entrenched oppression and institutional violence.

We are all believers and practitioners of nonviolence in human relationships. The challenge is to extend our belief and our practical skills to more difficult and remote situations of human conflict. Those who really commit themselves to these principles find that they work. Many lives are saved. Destruction is avoided, and everyone benefits as the process develops.

Our politicians often tell us that it is impossible to resolve conflicts without war. The fact is that they don't try hard enough, because it is our lives and our well being that they put on the line when they decide that violence is necessary.

6
Charity in the
Land of Individualism
by John D. Fargo

It was back on the farm, late 1940s, along the northwestern edge of the corn belt – in the land of individualism. Folks were poor, and only the more rugged had survived the ravages of the Great Depression, but times were better now.

A new farmer moved in and rented the farm across the section. I'll call him George. Within this self-reliant culture, George didn't fit in well. Each farm, a piece of carefully marked-off private property, was conscientiously cared for by the farmer and his family, but not George's.

This was before farmers used chemical weed killers. Thus, each farmer had to control weeds the hard way, by laboriously chopping them down, lest they go to seed and infest not only his fields but those of his neighbors. But not George.

We shared three-quarters of a mile of fence with George. Each farmer took care of half his common fences, making repairs when needed and chopping the weeds out of the fence row each summer. But George never laid a hand on any part of that fence.

Thistles were a nasty problem. Patches of these perennial weeds choked out the grain, and with no chemicals they were all but impossible to destroy. In the fall the thistles released thousands of tiny seeds that floated in the wind and could spread for miles. It was understood in the land of individualism that no one let his thistles go to seed – but George exempted himself. His farm became an eyesore in a culture where pride in one's property, rented or otherwise, ran high.

Farmers often had to extend themselves. For example, instead of the normal 12-hour workday, they might put in 15 to 18 hours a day to get the hay crop in before a rainstorm. But George was too irresponsible to put forth the extra effort.

Corn, which requires a relatively long growing season, was the main crop back then, but it was vulnerable along the northwestern edge of the corn belt. Farmers had no commercial grain driers; most of them didn't even have electricity. Thus, to prevent spoilage, the corn had to be left in the fields until it became sufficiently dry. This meant waiting until October, when early snows threatened to bury the crop.

Every October the race was on – to beat that first snowstorm and get the corn in. Corn-picking machines were repaired, greased, and ready to go. Corn cribs were built, farm kids skipped school to help with the harvest, and the time for 16-hour days, seven days a week, was on. But not George – his dilapidated corn picker wasn't ready. And his three little kids were too young to help bring in the crop.

Tragedy Strikes

Machinery was primitive by today's standards. Corn pickers often broke down, and dry corn husks often wouldn't feed down between the steel husking rollers. Instead, they accumulated above the rollers, plugging up the machine. The operator was constantly stopping his machine to dig out the jammed husks. It was a tedious process.

But there was a faster and easier way of handling this problem: leave the machine running, reach in with your hand, and push the husks down so they would feed through the steel-ridged rollers. It was dangerous; a man could lose his fingers.

Well, George did it the easy way. He had barely gotten started with his corn picking when those steel rollers grabbed his fingers. All the doctor could salvage of his mutilated right hand was part of one finger and his thumb, minus the nail.

"He probably deserved it." I never heard those words spoken, but I don't doubt that the thought ran through a mind or two. In any event, the forces of selection had weeded George out. Farming required a strong back and two good hands, and this incident ensured that George would never farm again.

Word of the tragedy spread rapidly. The next day, a neighbor drove up to where we were working and talked briefly to my father. The neighbor planned to work in George's fields the following day – maybe get some of his crop in – and thought we might like to help.

Early the next morning, we pulled into George's farm with our corn picker, wagons, elevator (a long conveyor mechanism that lifted the corn into the cribs), and hoist (which lifted the front end of the wagons for easier unloading). George had no permanent corn cribs, so we scrounged around in the dark, looking for pieces of old corn-crib fencing to construct temporary cribs. About then, another farmer pulled in with a trailer loaded with brand new corn-crib fencing.

Before daybreak, we had the elevator up and running, the bottom rung of the corn crib built, and the first loads of corn already were coming in from the fields. The bitter cold penetrated to the bone, and I was anxious to start unloading wagons.

A young farmer drove in with his corn picker, stopped where I was working, and asked if he could help me unload wagons. That seemed strange because running the elevator and hoist, tending the temperamental gasoline engine that powered the works, and unloading the wagons was normally a one-man job. He insisted until I convinced him that I could handle it – and they probably needed him and his corn picker in the fields.

It wasn't until he left that I realized it was probably my age that had prompted his offer. I was 11 or 12 at the time, but younger kids than I were operating the tractors that pulled the wagons loaded with corn.

Judging by the rate the corn started coming in, I figured there must have been a dozen corn pickers running. A second elevator pulled into the farmyard and was set up nearby. More corn pickers arrived – their faded yellow, green, or red paint showing through the dirt and grime of the machines. By mid-morning the place was swarming with people and machines.

Farm wives drove in with pots and baskets of food for dinner (the noon meal). The area near the farmhouse was beginning to look like a small parking lot. The house could not hold everyone, so we ate in shifts. Most ate quickly and quietly, then returned to work. I didn't know of anyone who was on "visiting terms" with George and his family.

By mid-afternoon, some of the corn pickers were returning from the fields, pulling through the farm yard, and leaving. One farmer, pulling in a load of corn, said that most of the corn was picked and they were starting to get in each other's way. Before dark George's entire crop was harvested, and he hadn't even returned from the hospital.

The remaining operators were solemnly departing. I counted over 20 corn pickers leaving, but there weren't that many farmers in the area. Some of them must have pulled their machines several miles in order to help out. Now, each farmer was going his own way, returning to his own fields where he would work late into the night in that annual race with the snowstorms.

That was how charity worked in the land of individualism, back before the welfare state became entrenched.

It may take the world a while, but eventually it will discover that true charity lies deep within the fertile soil of authentic individualism. These rugged souls, who dare to stand alone, tend to have hearts of gold.

Voluntaryist Resources

Books

The Ethics of Liberty, by **Murray Rothbard**

"First published in 1982, *The Ethics of Liberty* is a masterpiece of argumentation, and shockingly radical in its conclusions. Rothbard says that the very existence of the state – the entity with a monopoly privilege to invade private property – is contrary to the ethics of liberty. A society without a state is not only viable; it is the only one consistent with natural rights. In this volume, Rothbard first familiarizes the reader with Natural Law theory. After this ethical introduction, he goes on to address numerous ethical issues, showing how liberty is in the right in every case. In the final two sections, Rothbard enumerates the state's role in society as inherently anti-liberty, and details the structure of alternate theories of liberty." (Mises.org)

Our Enemy, The State, by **Albert J. Nock**

"What does one need to know about politics? In some ways, Nock has summed it all up in this astonishing book. Here was a prominent essayist at the height of the New Deal. In 1935, hardly any public intellectuals were making much sense at all. They pushed socialism. They pushed fascism. Everyone had a plan. Hardly anyone considered the possibility that the state was not fixing society but destroying it bit by bit. And so Albert Jay Nock came forward to write what needed to be written. And he ended up penning a classic of American political commentary, one that absolutely must be read by every student of economics and government." (Amazon.com)

I Must Speak Out, by **Carl Watner**

This work is "an Anthology of 70+ essays from the first 100 issues" of *The Voluntaryist* as published between 1982-1999.

Private Means, Public Ends by J. Wilson Mixon, Jr.

"This collection of essays daringly challenges the perceived wisdom of government necessity by pointing to instances of the free market fulfilling these functions. The book seeks to illustrate that there are, inevitably, many intrinsic problems with governmental attempts to plan and implement these functions. Moreover, governments operate on the leverage of coercion – whether that be in the form of laws or taxation. These essays suggest that the private alternatives not only tend to work better at achieving the desired end, but they also serve to reintroduce the much diminished principle upon which civil society is founded: namely voluntary cooperation between free men." (Amazon.com)

The Conscience of an Anarchist, by Gary Chartier

"Anarchy happens when people organize their lives peacefully and voluntarily – without the aggressive violence of the state. This simple but powerful book explains why the state is illegitimate, unnecessary, and dangerous, and what we can do to begin achieving real freedom." (Amazon.com)

The Economics and Ethics of Private Property by Hans Hoppe

"The right to private property is an indisputably valid, absolute principle of ethics, argues Hoppe, and the basis for civilizational advance. Indeed, it is the very foundation of social order itself. To rise from the ruins of socialism and overcome the stagnation of the Western welfare states, nothing will suffice but the uncompromising privatization of all socialized, that is, government, property and the establishment of a contractual society based on the recognition of private property rights." (Amazon.com)

Websites

FFF.org, "the mission of The Future of Freedom Foundation is to advance freedom by providing an uncompromising moral and economic case for individual liberty, free markets, and private property."

Voluntaryist.com is a website dedicated to promoting voluntaryism through the written word via an email group and newsletter, *The Voluntaryist*, and established by Carl Watner. From their Statement of Purpose, "Voluntaryists are advocates of non-political, non-violent strategies to achieve a free society. We reject electoral politics, in theory and in practice, as incompatible with libertarian principles. Governments must cloak their actions in an aura of moral legitimacy in order to sustain their power, and political methods invariably strengthen that legitimacy. Voluntaryists seek instead to delegitimize the State through education, and we advocate withdrawal of the cooperation and tacit consent on which State power ultimately depends."

LewRockwell.com is the most read libertarian website in the world. From their About page, "The daily news and opinion site LewRockwell.com was founded in 1999 by anarcho-capitalists Lew Rockwell and Burt Blumert to help carry on the anti-war, anti-state, pro-market work of Murray N. Rothbard."

C4SS.org, "The Center for a Stateless Society is a project of the Molinari Institute and dedicated to building public awareness of, and support for, market anarchism. We provide news commentary, related analysis and original research from our unique perspective, serving as a market anarchist *media center.*"

Praxeology.net/molinari.htm, "The mission of the Molinari Institute is to promote understanding of the philosophy of Market Anarchism as a sane, consensual alternative to the hypertrophic violence of the State. The Institute takes its name from Gustave de Molinari (1819-1912), originator of the theory of Market Anarchism."

CompleteLiberty.com is a website "for those who advocate complete liberty, to share ideas and create and join local groups, devising win/win strategies to help people and institutions evolve to the truly free market society of the future." Created by Wes Bertrand.

Strike-The-Root.com "is a daily journal of current events and commentary from a libertarian/market anarchist perspective. The mission of STR is to advance the cause of liberty, primarily by de-mystifying and de-legitimizing the State. STR seeks a world where people are free to live their lives as they see fit, as long as they don't use force or fraud against peaceful people."

ZeroGov.com is a website dedicated to setting people "free from the physical and intellectual shackles that makes them wards of the state and beasts of burden subject to the whim of rulers whose only legitimacy is the perception by the fettered and the chained that they must submit."

Section Two – Religion

7
The Origin of Religious Tolerance
by Wendy McElroy

In 1733 the philosopher credited with ushering in the French Enlightenment, François Marie Arouet de Voltaire, published *Letters Concerning the English Nation*. It was a pivotal work. Although written in French, the 24 letters were first issued from London in an English translation; the material was considered too politically dangerous for the author or any French printer to have the work appear in France.*

Voltaire was no stranger to such controversy. Some years before, after being beaten up by the hirelings of an aristocrat whom he had offended, Voltaire had been thrown into the Bastille (for the second time). He was released after pledging to stay at least 50 leagues away from Paris. Voltaire chose to go as far as England, where he stayed for roughly two-and-a-half years. The result of the sojourn was the *Letters* on English religion and politics, written as though to explain English society to a friend back in France. They finally appeared in France in 1734 as *Lettres philosophiques*, or *Philosophical Letters*.

*For citations, see: http://goo.gl/Y2s4t

Letter five, "On the Church of England," began with the observation, "This is the country of sects. An Englishman, as a freeman, goes to Heaven by whatever road he pleases." The statement had profound implications for any citizen of France – a nation that had almost destroyed itself in order to establish Catholicism as the only practiced religion.

In the next paragraph, Voltaire pursued a theme that contributed heavily to the danger of publishing his work in France: he examined the intellectual and institutional foundation of England's religious tolerance. First, he rejected a political explanation. Referring to the established Church of England, he acknowledged that politics strongly favored prejudice rather than tolerance. He wrote, "No one can hold office in England or in Ireland unless he is a faithful Anglican."* Such political exclusion hardly promoted religious good will.

Nor did the religious preaching of the dominant church lead the nation toward toleration. According to Voltaire, the Anglican clergy worked "up in their flocks as much holy zeal against nonconformists as possible." Yet in recent decades, the "fury of the sects... went no further than sometimes breaking the windows of heretical chapels."

What, then, accounted for the extreme religious toleration in the streets of London as compared to those of Paris?

The Peace of Commerce

In letter six, "On the Presbyterians," Voltaire ascribed the "peace" in which "they [Englishmen] lived happily together" to a mechanism that was a pure expression of the free market – the London Stock Exchange. In the most famous passage from *Philosophical Letters*, Voltaire observed, "Go into the Exchange in London, that place more venerable than many a court, and you will see representatives of all the nations assembled there for the profit of mankind. There the Jew, the Mahometan, and the Christian deal with one another as if they were of the same religion, and reserve the name of infidel for those who go bankrupt."

Legally and historically, England was no bastion of religious toleration: laws against nonconformists and atheists were still in force. Yet in England, and not in France, there was an air of toleration on the street that existed quite apart from the law. Even though both countries had aristocracies, England was not burdened with the unyielding class structure that crippled social and economic mobility in France. As Voltaire wrote in letter nine, "On the Government": "You hear no talk in this country [England] of high, middle, and low justice, nor of the right of hunting over the property of a citizen who himself has not the liberty of firing a shot in his own field."

A key to the difference between England and France lay in the English system of commerce and in the comparatively high regard in which the English held their merchants. (This is not meant to slight the substantial differences between the English and French governments – especially the constitutional ones – upon which Voltaire dwelled.) In France, aristocrats and the other elites of society regarded those in commerce with unalloyed contempt. In letter 10, "On Commerce," Voltaire pointedly commented on the French attitude: "The merchant himself so often hears his profession spoken of disdainfully that he is fool enough to blush." Yet in England, the "merchant justly proud" compares himself "not without some reason, to a Roman citizen." Indeed, the younger sons of nobility often entered commerce or took up a profession. This difference in attitude was a large factor in explaining the extraordinary rise of the English middle class, their wealth deriving from trade. Indeed, the French often derided England as a nation of shopkeepers. Voltaire thought this was a compliment, observing that if the English were able to sell themselves, it proved that they were worth something.

Commerce, or shop-keeping, established an arena within which people dealt with each other solely for economic benefit and, so, ignored extraneous factors such as the other party's religious practices. On the floor of the London Stock Exchange, religious differences disappeared into background noise as people scrambled to make a profit from one another. The economic self-interest of the Christian and the Jew outweighed the prejudice that might otherwise sour personal relations between them. They intersected and cooperated on a point of common interest: "the Presbyterian trusts the Anabaptist, and the Church of England man accepts the promise of the Quaker," Voltaire wrote in "On the Presbyterians."

Voltaire Versus Marx

Ironically, Voltaire singled out for praise precisely the same aspect of commerce – the London Stock Exchange – that Karl Marx later condemned. Both viewed the marketplace as impersonal or, in more negative Marxist terms, dehumanizing. For Marx, people in the marketplace ceased to be individuals expressing their humanity and became interchangeable units who bought and sold. To Voltaire, the impersonal nature of trade was a good thing. It allowed people to disregard the divisive human factors that had historically disrupted society, such as differences of religion and class. The very fact that a Christian who wished to profit from a Jew, and vice versa, had to disregard the personal characteristics of the other party and deal with him civilly was what recommended the London Stock Exchange to Voltaire.

In this, Voltaire's voice is reminiscent of Adam Smith in his most popular work, *The Wealth of Nations*. Smith outlined how everyone in a civilized market society is dependent on the cooperation of multitudes even though his friends may number no more than a dozen or so. A marketplace requires the participation of throngs of people, most of whom one never directly encounters. It would be folly for any man to expect multitudes of strangers to benefit him out of sheer benevolence or because they like him. The cooperation of the butcher or the brewer, said Smith, was ensured by their simple self-interest. Thus, those who entered the marketplace did not need the approval or favor of those with whom they dealt. They needed only to pay their bills.

The toleration created by the London Stock Exchange extended far beyond its doors. After conducting business with each other, the Christian and the Jew went their separate ways. As Voltaire phrased it, "On leaving these peaceable and free assemblies, some go to the synagogue, others in search of a drink..." In the end, "all are satisfied."

The *Philosophical Letters* – Voltaire's tribute to the English middle class, their commerce, and their society – created an enormous impact on the European intellectual scene. Calling the work "a declaration of war and a map of campaign," Will and Ariel Durant commented: "Rousseau said of these letters that they played a large part in the awakening of his mind; there must have been thousands of young Frenchmen who owed the book a similar debt. Lafayette said it made him a republican at the age of nine. [Heinrich] Heine thought 'it was not necessary for the censor to condemn this book; it would have been read without that.'"*

The French Reaction

Nevertheless, French censors seemed eager to condemn it. The printer was imprisoned in the Bastille. A *lettre de cachet* for the elusive Voltaire's immediate arrest was issued. By a legislative order, all known copies of the work were confiscated and burned in front of the Palais de Justice. Through the intercession of powerful friends, the *lettre de cachet* was withdrawn, again on the promise that he remain safely outside the limits of Paris. In this manner did the French church and state respond to Voltaire's salute to toleration.

But the themes of the *Philosophical Letters* resounded deeply within the consciousness of Europe for many decades to come. One of its themes was that freedom – especially freedom of commerce – was the true wellspring of religious toleration and of a peaceful civil society. The insight was nothing short of revolutionary because it reversed the accepted argument and policies on how to create a harmonious society. Traditionally, France (along with most other European nations) attempted to enforce a homogeneous system of values on its people in the belief that common values were necessary to ensure peace and harmony, the social glue that held together the social fabric. This was thought to be particularly true of religious values.

This was not a moral argument, but a practical one: society would collapse into open violence without the cohesion provided by common values. Thus, those in authority needed to centrally plan and rigorously enforce the values that should be taught to and should be practiced by the masses. After all, if people were allowed to choose their own religious values, if values became a commodity open to competition, then civil chaos and conflict would inevitably ensue.

Voltaire argued that precisely the opposite was true. The process of imposing homogeneous values led only to conflict and religious wars. The result was a society intellectually stagnant and morally corrupt, because doubt or dissent was suppressed. It was diversity and freedom that created a thriving and peaceful society. Voltaire ended his most-quoted letter, "On the Presbyterians," by observing: "If there were only one religion in England, there would be danger of tyranny; if there were two, they would cut each other's throats; but there are thirty, and they live happily together in peace."

Perhaps one reason that Voltaire's *Philosophical Letters* created such a backlash from the French leviathan was that the book's logic, if carried beyond religion, would strike at any government attempt to impose common values or practices on the people. Indeed, Voltaire's argument against homogeneity continues to have deep implications for the centralized policies of all governments. Those citizens who reject imposed homogeneity in religion might well be prompted to question the wisdom of many other government institutions, including public schools, which are often justified by the declared need for common values. The freedom of individuals to decide matters of value for themselves could easily prompt them to demand the right to live according to those values and to teach them to their children. Thus could the system of centralized control unravel.

8

The Historical Origins of Voluntaryism

by James Luther Adams

In modern history the first crucial affirmation of voluntaryism as an institutional phenomenon appeared in the demand of the sects for the separation of church and state. In England, for example, and then later in America, the intention was to do away with direct state control of the church and also to remove official ecclesiastical influence from the political realm, toward the end of creating a voluntary church. In the voluntary church, religious faith as well as membership was to be a matter of individual choice. The individual was no longer automatically to become a member of the church simply by reason of his being born in the territory. Moreover, he could choose not to be a member of a church. Nor was rejection of the established confession any longer to be considered a political offense or to deprive the unbeliever of the civil franchise. In rejecting state control, the church (and the theological seminary) were no longer to be supported by taxation. The objection to taxation in support of the church was two-fold: tax support, it was held, not only gave the state some right of control; it also represented a way of coercing the nonmember or the un-believer to give financial support to the church. Freedom of choice for the individual brought with it another freedom, namely, the freedom to parti-cipate in the shaping of the policies of the church group of his choice. The rationale for this voluntaryism was worked out theologically by the sec-tarians of the sixteenth and seventeenth centuries, and more in terms of so-cial and political theory by John Locke in the next century.

From the point of view of a theory of associations, the demand for the separation of church and state and the emergence of the voluntary church represent the end of an old era and the beginning of a new one. The earlier era had been dominated by the ideal of "Christendom," a unified structure of society in a church-state. In the new era, the voluntary church, the free church, no longer supported by taxation, was to be self-sustaining; and it was to manage its own affairs. In the earlier era, kinship, caste, and res-tricted community groups had determined most of the interests and the forms of participation. In the new era these interests became segregated. In this respect the freedom of choice was increased. The divorce of church and state and the advent of freedom of religious association illustrate this type of increase in freedom of choice.

In accord with this new conception of religious freedom and respon-sibility one must view the collection plate in the church service on Sunday as a symbol of the meaning of disestablishment and of voluntaryism. The collection plate symbolizes – indeed it in part also actualizes and ins-titutionalizes – the view that the church, as a corporate body, is a self-de-terminative group and that in giving financial support to the church the members affirm responsibility to participate in the shaping of the policies of the church. Thus the voluntary principle amounts to the principle of con-sent. One must add, however, that although the struggle for voluntaryism on a large scale in the church began over two hundred and fifty years ago, it was not achieved generally and officially in the United States until the nineteenth century – that is, apart from the colonies that from the be-ginning had had no establishment.

The thrust toward the separation of church and state could succeed only by carrying through a severe struggle for freedom of association. Initially, the authorities who opposed it asserted that the health of society was threatened by the voluntary principle. They held that uniformity of belief was a prerequisite of a viable social order. As a separation of powers, voluntaryism was viewed as a wedge for chaos. In order to defend the unrestricted sovereignty of the commonwealth, Thomas Hobbes published in 1651 *Leviathan*, the most cogent attack of the times upon the voluntary principle. In his view the church should be only an arm of the sovereign. Indeed, no association of any sort was to exist apart from state control. Therefore he spoke of voluntary associations, religious or secular, as "worms in the entrails of the natural man" (the integrated social whole). Analogous attacks upon the voluntary church came also from conservatives in the American colonies where establishment prevailed.

Hobbes recognized that freedom of religious association would bring in its train the demand for other freedoms of association. His fears were fully justified. Indeed, with the emergence of this multiple conception of freedom of association a new conception of society came to birth - that of the pluralistic, the multi-group society.

9
For Conscience's Sake
by Carl Watner

George Smith, in his essay "Philosophies of Toleration," reviews the history of freedom of religion and identifies the moral axiom of "righteous persecution," which has been part of most religions throughout the ages. The principle underlying this "persecution complex" was that recalcitrant people should be coerced "for their own good." It made no difference whether people were being compelled to change their earthly behavior or their spiritual beliefs. The justification for persecution was the same in either case: the end – the public welfare in the here-and-now or the salvation of the persecuted in the hereafter – warranted the use of violence. The opposite proposition, based on the principle of persuasion, embraced the voluntaryist prescription for reasonable argument and non-violent behavior. Many defenders of religious freedom understood that force could only make hypocrites of men, or as William Penn put it, "tis only persuasion that makes (true) converts."

An interesting twist on Smith's comments about persecution is to apply them to the ancient practice of State taxation. Since taxation is the taking of another's property by the public authorities without his voluntary consent, clearly taxation may be viewed as a form of persecution by those who would not willingly pay. Indeed, William McLoughlin described "the principal aspect of the struggle against the Puritan establishment" in America as "the effort to abolish compulsory tax support for any and all denominations." If it is correct to characterize religious taxes as coercive and as a form of persecution, then it should certainly be proper to categorize other forms of taxation similarly. The principle at work is the same regardless of the purpose behind the tax. Property must be forcibly taken from some people and applied in ways which they (the owners) would not ordinarily direct it.

Seventeenth and eighteenth century advocates of toleration, like Henry Robinson, William Penn, John Locke, and James Madison, all viewed "freedom of conscience" as a form of property. Robinson claimed that "those who are forced to pay a (religious) fine are subject to a forcing of their conscience." Penn often argued that to punish religious dissent by fines and imprisonment was as much an invasion of conscience as it was of property rights. Locke in *A Letter Concerning Toleration* called "liberty of conscience... every man's natural right." Madison, in his essay on "Property," wrote that "Conscience is the most sacred of all property..." So it was clearly recognized that religious persecution took on many forms – from being compelled to pay taxes to support a minister one did not patronize, to the confiscation of property for the non-payment of such taxes, to the actual imprisonment of the persecuted minorities who insisted on practicing their religion publicly or refusing to falsely swear their allegiance to a king or god of whom their conscience would not approve.

The entire basis on which religious taxes were laid was the idea that "the authority of the church (wa)s as essential to the continued existence of civil society as that of the (S)tate." It was assumed that religion would not be able to sustain itself without some financial assistance from the State. "Thus," as McLoughlin writes,

> "the controversy over the establishment of religion in America in
> 1780 was not over the establishment of any one sect, denomination or
> creed, but over the establishment of religion in general (meaning, the

Protestant religion). The question of support for religion was often compared to the responsibility of the state toward all institutions concerning the general welfare – the courts, the roads, the schools, the armed forces. If justice, commerce, education, religion, peace were essential to the general welfare, then ought these not to be supported out of general taxation? It was no more inconsistent in the minds of most New Englanders to require a general tax for the support of religion than to require, as Jefferson advocated, a general tax for the creation and maintenance of a public school system."*

The purpose of this essay is to demonstrate the uniqueness of the voluntaryist argument for religious freedom. The voluntaryist does not advocate separation of Church and State because the issue is a red herring. To argue for separation of Church and State does nothing more than to legitimize the State since it does not question or challenge the State's existence. The issue, by the nature of the way it is framed, assumes that the State must and should exist. The fact of the matter is that Church and State will never truly be separated until either one or the other disappears. Tax exemption of church property or taxation of church property? So long as a State engages in compulsory taxation to raise its revenue, it must inevitably impact on the religious sphere. Has the religionist, who must support the police with his taxes, had his rights violated when the police come to the aid of the atheist? If the State pays a policeman to direct traffic and protect children going to church schools, might not the atheist object to having his tax money spent in such a fashion? Only a voluntaryist would recognize the injustice inherent in these situations. So long as the State violates property rights by its existence – which it must necessarily do – religious freedom or any other form of freedom will never be secure. In principle and in practice, all freedoms are interrelated to one other. If a property right may be violated in one sphere, by the same principle it may be violated in another.

---

*For citations, see: http://goo.gl/dHDYz

The balance of this essay will discuss the issues of toleration, religious freedom, separation of Church and State, and freedom of conscience from the voluntaryist point of view.

Liberty not Toleration

Religious liberty or freedom of conscience, as the early dissenters called it, means thinking as one pleases, and then using one's body and rightfully owned property to express those thoughts without being coercively molested. For example, religious freedom manifests itself in the right to build places of worship, to print religious literature, to speak of one's ideas without the possibility of physical retaliation, and the right not to have ones property taken or used in ways that the rightful owner deems inappropriate. Yet, no historical religious thinker ever thoroughly understood the principle behind religious liberty. A religious radical, like Roger Williams, saw that it was wrong to "steal" a person's property to support a religion he did not practice. Yet no supporter of religious liberty ever questioned the propriety of compulsory taxation as it applied to the secular realm.

The English dissenters of the late 18th Century, however, did go so far as to support the individual against the collective, no matter what form the issue took. For them, freedom of conscience was "a principle implicit in human nature, a right innate in the heart of every man, constituting the essence of personality..." Writing about the dissenters' view of freedom of conscience, Anthony Lincoln says:

> "It implied that there were certain issues so fundamental that no municipal laws or conventions, no social or conventional machinery, could compass or even approach them, but could be resolved only in the reason and conscience of the individual: an inner sanctuary into which all commands of priest and magistrates penetrated only as idle, meaningless echoes."*

In his 1837 sermon on "Intellectual Liberty," Reverend Horatio Potter described the principle which lies at the foundation of the right to freedom of conscience as one which is at the very basis of all intellectual and religious liberty. It is an epistemological bias against violence which, he said, is predicated on the premise that "error is to be refuted, that truth is to be made manifest and its influence extended not by external force, but by reasoning... Produce your strong reasons – employ your intellect to shew wherein my intellect has erred or led others into error, but abstain from violence, which can prove only that you are powerful and vindictive, without proving that you have truth and justice on your side." The resort to violence is a confession of weakness because he who would employ force would not do so unless his arguments and reasoning were weak and unconvincing. Truth or the effort to obtain the truth does not need to rely on force. "If a man believes he possesses the truth, then let him convince others by argument, not compel them by threats."

Henry Robinson (1605-1664), along with other Englishmen of his age such as John Milton, John Lilburne, and Richard Overton, were among the first of the moderns to see that the idea that violence was not a convincing argument (and hence compulsion should not be threatened or used in order to bring about a change of opinion) applied just as much to the economic and political realm as it did to the religious sphere. In his book, *Liberty of Conscience*, published in 1643, Robinson brought forth just about every "argument that the modern world has been able to advance in defense of religious liberty." The right of private judgment or freedom of conscience, as Robinson identified it, was as much an individual right as the right to life, liberty, or property. None of these rights were secure so long as people could be imprisoned, fined, and coerced for their religious or political beliefs. In fact, Robinson compared the freedom to choose one's religion to the freedom to engage in free enterprise activities. As William Haller explained, Robinson argued that since "no man has a monopoly on truth" in any sphere of life,

> "'the more freely each man exercises his own gifts in its pursuit, the
> more of truth will be discovered and possessed.' As 'in civil affairs... ,
> every man most commonly understands his own business,' as 'every

man is desirous to do with his own as he thinks good himself,' and as it would be absurd for the State to make laws requiring men to manage their worldly affairs after one 'general prescript forme and manner,' so in religion every man should be permitted to go his own way. Compulsion compels men only to hypocrisy or rebellion."*

Although the distinction was not articulated until the following century, Robinson and others of his era could see that there was a difference between religious toleration and religious liberty. The voluntaryist argues for the latter, while the statist implicitly endorses the former. The difference is that what the State at one time tolerates, it may, at another time, condemn and prohibit. Hence, whatever freedom of activity is granted by toleration is subject to restriction and/or revocation. "Toleration is not the *opposite* of intolerance, but is the *counterfeit* of it," wrote Thomas Paine in 1791 in *The Rights of Man*. Religious liberty, no more than the liberty to own property, is not granted by anyone or any institution. It precedes the organization of the State and arises from the nature of man and the manner in which he best lives. Freedom of religion was "a right so sacred" that Mirabeau once explained to the French Constituent Assembly that the word "toleration" seems to "convey a suggestion of tyranny." He pointed out that "the existence of any authority which has the power to tolerate is an encroachment upon the liberty of thought, precisely because it tolerates and therefore has the power not to tolerate."

J.B. Bury in his *A History of Freedom of Thought* (1913) surveyed the many different approaches to intellectual liberty throughout the ages, but they all ultimately reduce themselves to the fact that the coercion of opinion is never successful, and that "reasons' only weapon" has been logical "argument." Since the beginning of written history, one can probably find people who "refused to be coerced by any human authority or tribunal into a course which his own mind condemned as wrong." The conflict between the individual and the collective (whatever form the latter took) is simply a replay of the eternal struggle for the supremacy of individual conscience over man-made statutes.

Religion and Citizenship

Two historical observations become apparent as one reviews the history of arguments and the actual struggle for religious liberty. First of all, those who were in fact persecuted, such as the early Christians or the latter-day Puritans, often resorted to persecution themselves, once they attained political power. "Courageous dissenters often became intolerant conformists." The advocates of religious liberty sometimes themselves "practiced religious discrimination." The corruptive influence of political power often manifested itself in such contradictory ways. The other historical observation is that those who supported a tolerant or *laissez faire* attitude toward religious beliefs always thought that man's religious beliefs were of no harm or consequence to anyone else. The Roman emperor Tiberius (43 B.C.-37 A.D.) said that, "If the Gods are insulted, let them see to it (the punishment of the blasphemers) themselves." Tertullian (145-225), an early Christian, took the position that one man's religion can neither hurt nor help another. More modern thinkers embraced the same idea. Martin Luther (1483-1546) – before changing his opinion – defended freedom of religion by declaring that "everyone [should] believe what he likes." Montaigne, Luther's contemporary, once remarked that "It is setting a high value on one's opinions to roast men on account of them." A century latter, John Locke as much said that, "If false beliefs are an offense to God, it is really his affair." And Frederick the Great, writing in 1740, a few months after his accession to the throne, noted "that everyone should be allowed to go to heaven in his own way."

What all these thinkers, and a great number of others not mentioned, shared was the belief that "the right of private judgment must be given free scope and every man, being completely responsible for his own soul, must seek and find the truth in his own way." For them, "the right to seek the truth in one's own way" comprises one of the most important and necessary responsibilities of life. Under normal circumstances, whatever faith a person might profess is irrelevant to his status as a good citizen. The problem is that often times the demands of good citizenship can conflict with the demands of one's religion. Thus Marcus Aurelius, one of the most enlightened and stoical of the Roman emperors, persecuted Christians "because they refused to recognize the sacred character of" his position, "a refusal which threatened to undermine the foundations of the state." Centuries later, the Anabaptists were persecuted because they denied the Magistrate's right to use force, and hence called into question their "right to exist at all." John W. Allen in his *A History of Political Thought in the Sixteenth Century* (1928) pointed out:

"...It was mainly on the ground of their denial of rightful jurisdiction in the magistrate that they were everywhere persecuted... They were persecuted as anarchists rather than as heretics. But theirs was a religious anarchism: and it was just this fact that made the problem of dealing with them a difficult one for Protestant governments inclined to toleration. To say that they were condemned as anarchists was, really, simply to suppress part of the truth; since it could be shown that their anarchism was one with their religious opinions. We prate religious toleration as though it rested on some principle of universal validity. But religious toleration may be inconsistent with the maintenance of government."*

In the Netherlands... Menno Simons (1492-1559) taught,

"...(the Anabaptists that) (t)he faithful must refuse any military service. If they really held that the use of force was in all cases unlawful... they were logically bound not to accept it (military service and the coercive government which it supported). They were bound, indeed, to refuse to pay taxes at all to support the evil thing."*

Consequently, what was a State to do if it was faced with a large portion of its populace, who refused to serve in the military or pay taxes to support its activities (military or otherwise)? Historically and theoretically, if the State was to continue its State-like functions, it must not and could not tolerate such behavior. Few would serve or pay if conscientious objection to military service and taxation were an integral part of its legal structure.

The British colonies and early American states were faced with this dilemma. For example, the New England Baptists claimed for themselves the same principle which the American revolutionists used to justify their separation from the mother country. Isaac Backus, leader of the New England Baptists, repeatedly used the argument that "the Baptist grievances... were much more serious than the three-penny tax on tea, which anyone could avoid by abstaining from drinking tea." The Baptists thought that they had as much right to seek liberty of conscience (and freedom from religious taxes which they vigorously opposed) in Massachusetts as Americans did to seek civil liberty from Parliament in England. Baptists were repeatedly jailed and had their goods auctioned off for non-payment of religious taxes.

The basic premise behind the imprisonment of Baptists and other dissenters was that civil cohesion could not exist without religious unity. Many Americans reject this premise today, because we have 200 years of "cohesive" nationalism behind us, but the situation in the early 1790s was not so clear. Although the drafters of the federal Constitution confirmed the lack of federal jurisdiction over religion, the fact is that in 1789, when James Madison proposed an amendment to the federal Constitution "prohibiting the states from violating certain rights, including freedom of religion, the House of Representatives approved of Madison's proposal but the Senate voted it down." The "representatives" of the people were not so sure that individuals, rather than the states, could be trusted with responsibility for their own religious freedom.

The Massachusetts Constitution of 1780

The contradictory and inconsistent reception of Church and State "separation" in the early American states is well documented in the case of Massachusetts. Under Article II of its Constitution of 1780, Massachusetts recognized:

> "It is the right as well as the duty of all men in society, publicly, and at stated seasons, to worship the Supreme Being, the great Creator and Preserver of the universe. And no subject shall be hurt, molested, or re-

strained, in his person, liberty, or estate for worshipping God in the manner and season most agreeable to the dictates of his own conscience; or for his religious profession or sentiments; provided he doth not disturb the public peace, or obstruct others in their religious worship."

But Article III of the same document practically denied religious freedom to non-believers and believers in non-protestant faiths in the state:

"As the happiness of a people, and the good order and preservation of civil government, essentially depend upon piety, religion, and morality; and as these cannot be generally diffused through a community but by the institution of the public worship of GOD, and of public instruction in piety, religion, and morality: Therefore, to promote their happiness, and to secure the good order and preservation of their government, the people of this commonwealth have a right to invest their legislature with the power to authorize and require, and the legislature shall... authorize and require, the several towns, parishes, precincts, and other bodies politic, or religious societies, to make suitable provision, at their own expense, for the institution of public worship of GOD, and for the support and maintenance of public Protestant teachers of piety, religion, and morality..." (The article then continues, giving the legislature power to compel attendance for the purpose of religious instruction, and the power to coercively assess all citizens of the state for the support of public teachers of religion.)

The controversy over the passage and ratification of the Massachusetts Constitution of 1780 has been documented by modern-day historians, such as Oscar and Mary Handlin and William McLoughlin. The latter found that Article III "was the only one in the entire constitution which did not receive the necessary two-thirds vote for approval." Those who tabulated the votes "were able by careful juggling of the statistics, to make it appear as though it had." The returns from towns which actually opposed Article III, but offered an amendment to it, were counted in favor of the existing article, rather than opposed to it.

Middleborough, one of the towns that opposed Article III, protested that it "might compel individuals under some circumstances to pay money contrary to the dictates of their consciences." The citizens of West Springfield, Massachusettes, explained that if the legislature had the power to compel citizens to attend public worship "at stated times and seasons," then it could "prohibit the worship of God at any other time... and also define what worship shall be and so the right of private Judgement will be at an end." One letter writer during the campaign summed up the opposition in the following manner. A person signing himself "Philanthropos," wrote that "The third article is repugnant to and destructive of the second... The second says the people shall be free, and the third says they shall not be free... To use an old saying [Articles II and III are] like a cow that gives a full pail of milk and then kicks it over."

The supporters of Article III believed that if the restraints on religion were broken down by not compelling religious attendance or support, then it would be hopeless to "preserve the order and government of the state." The "trouble with allowing anyone to exempt himself from religious taxes on grounds of liberty of conscience" was that "the most abandoned wretch who has no conscience at all and is too avaricious to do anything... has only to say that he is conscientiously against" public worship and religious taxation. "The pretended proposal grants full liberty to every man to have no conscience at all, and to be as deceitful and hypocritical as he pleases." The most daring argument for Article III went so far as to claim that its opponents wanted "to deprive a respectable part of the community of what they esteemed a right of conscience, viz., the right of supporting public worship and the teachers of religion by law." In a stunning reversal of natural rights thinking, the supporters of Article III believed that the community at large had the right to tax and control everyone under their jurisdiction. Hence, the loss of this power would be a violation of the consciences of those who advocated religious taxes.

The Baptists, Universalists, Quakers, Shakers, Episcopalians, and Methodists were all sects that opposed Article III, and suffered by its enforcement. Despite the provisions of Article II, the seizure and confiscation of private property of religious believers took place. Some constitutional test cases were taken to court, but none were successful in overturning Article III. Theophilius Parsons, a member of the committee that drew up Article III, wrote a judicial opinion when he was Chief Justice of the Supreme Judicial Court of Massachusetts in 1810, that explained its rationale. He wrote that since "every citizen derives the security of his property and the fruits of his industry, from the power of the state, so as the price of this protection he is bound to contribute in common with his fellow-citizens for the public use, so much of his property and for such public uses as the state shall direct... The distinction between *liberty of conscience and worship, and the right of appropriating money,* is material; the former is unalienable, the latter is surrendered as the price of protection. Religious teaching is to enforce the moral duties and thereby protection of persons and property."

To the objection that it is "intolerant to compel a man to pay for religious instruction from which as he does not hear it, he can derive no benefit," Parsons answered that, "The like objection may be made by any man to the support of public schools, if he has no family who attends; and any man who has no lawsuit may object to the support of judges and jurors on the same ground." Religious instruction supports "correct morals among the people" and cultivates "just habits and manners, by which every man's person and property are protected from outrage and his personal and social enjoyments promoted."

Almost two hundred years after Parsons wrote these words, we find that his arguments are still used to justify statism. The safety of the State and the preservation of the general welfare both require public taxation. Without money to fund itself, the State could not provide for the security of private property (as though private property is ever secure when subject to the depredations of the State). In a sort of perverse way, those who supported religious taxation in America during the late 18th and early 19th centuries were at least consistent in their reasoning. They realized the "virus" of voluntaryism (whether religious or secular), could undermine the foundation of the State. If the general welfare could be best served by permitting each individual to follow his own self-interest, then this argument should apply as much to the religious sphere as to the economic realm. Just as religious liberty is more than a fight for religion, so economic liberty is more than a fight for free economic transactions. Both are part of the struggle for liberty in all spheres of life. Just as religion flourishes best when left to private voluntary support, so do economic transactions, protection of property, and the settlement of disputes. The "virus" of voluntaryism is contagious and consistent. It leaves no stone unturned; it applies to all the affairs of people, whether public or private. It leaves no room for the State or coercion.

10
Secular Theocracy
by David J. Theroux

Part 1

We live in an increasingly secularized world of massive and pervasive nation states in which traditional religion, especially Christianity, is ruled unwelcome and even a real danger on the basis of a purported history of intolerance and "religious violence." This is found in most all "public" domains, including the institutions of education, business, government, welfare, transportation, parks and recreation, science, art, foreign affairs, economics, entertainment, and the media. A secularized public square policed by government is viewed as providing a neutral, rational, free, and safe domain that keeps the "irrational" forces of religion from creating conflict and darkness. And we are told that real progress requires expanding this domain by pushing religion ever backward into remote corners of society where it has little or no influence. In short, modern America has become a secular theocracy with a civic religion of national politics (nationalism) occupying the public realm in which government has replaced God.

For the renowned Christian scholar and writer C.S. Lewis, such a view was fatally flawed morally, intellectually, and spiritually, producing the twentieth-century rise of the total state, total war, and mega-genocides. For Lewis, Christianity provided the one true and coherent worldview that applied to *all* human aspirations and endeavors: "I believe in Christianity as I believe that the sun has risen, not only because I see it, but because by it I see everything else."*

In his book, *The Discarded Image*, Lewis revealed that for Medieval Christians, there was no sacred/secular divide and that this unified, theo-political worldview of hope, joy, liberty, justice, and purpose from the loving grace of God enabled them to discover the objective, natural-law principles of ethics, science, and theology, producing immense human flourishing.* Lewis described the natural law as a cohesive and interconnected objective standard of right behavior:

"This thing which I have called for convenience the *Tao*, and which others may call Natural Law or Traditional Morality or the First Principles of Practical Reason or the First Platitudes, is not one among a series of possible systems of value. It is *the* sole source of all value judgements. If it is rejected, all values are rejected. If any value is retained, it is retained. The effort to refute it and raise a new system of value in its place is self-contradictory. There has never been, and never will be, a radically new judgement of value in the history of the world. What purport to be new systems or (as they now call them) 'ideologies,' all consist of fragments from the *Tao* itself. Arbitrarily wrenched from their context in the whole and then swollen to madness in their isolation, yet still owing to the *Tao* and to it alone such validity as they possess. If my duty to my parents is a superstition, then so is my duty to posterity. If justice is a superstition, then so is my duty to my country or my race. If the pursuit of scientific knowledge is a real value, then so is conjugal fidelity."*

And in his recent book, *The Victory of Reason*, Rodney Stark has further shown "How Christianity Led to Freedom, Capitalism, and the Success

---

*For citations, see: http://goo.gl/AvBfE

of the West."* Similarly and prior to the rise of the secular nation-state in America, Alexis de Tocqueville documented in his 1835 volume, *Democracy in America*, the remarkable flexibility, vitality and cohesion of Christian-rooted liberty in American society with business enterprises, churches and aid societies, covenants and other private institutions and communities.*

In his book, *The Myth of Religious Violence: Secular Ideology and the Roots of Modern Conflict*, William Cavanaugh similarly notes that for Augustine and the ancient world, religion was not a distinct realm separate from the secular. The origin of the term "religion" (*religio*) came from Ancient Rome (*re-ligare*, to rebind or relink) as a serious obligation for a person in the natural law ("*religio* for me") not only at a shrine, but also in civic oaths and family rituals that most westerners would today consider secular. In the Middle Ages, Aquinas further viewed *religio* not as a set of private beliefs but instead a devotion toward moral excellence in *all* spheres.*

However in the Renaissance, religion became viewed as a "private" impulse, distinct from "secular" politics, economics, and science.* This "modern" view of religion began the decline of the church as the public, communal practice of the virtue of *religio*. And by the Enlightenment, John Locke had distinguished between the "outward force" of civil officials and the "inward persuasion" of religion. He believed that civil harmony required a strict division between the state, whose interests are "public," and the church, whose interests are "private," thereby clearing the public square for the purely secular. For Locke, the church is a "voluntary society of men," but obedience to the state is mandatory.*

The subsequent rise of the modern state in claiming a monopoly on violence, lawmaking, and public allegiance within a given territory depended upon either absorbing the church into the state or relegating the church to a private realm. As Cavanaugh notes:

> "Key to this move is the contention that the church's business is religion. Religion must appear, therefore, not as what the church is left

with once it has been stripped of earthly relevance, but as the timeless and essential human endeavor to which the church's pursuits should always have been confined... In the wake of the Reformation, princes and kings tended to claim authority over the church in their realms, as in Luther's Germany and Henry VIII's England... The new conception of religion helped to facilitate the shift to state dominance over the church by distinguishing inward religion from the bodily disciplines of the state."*

For Enlightenment figures like Jean-Jacques Rousseau who dismissed natural law, "civic religion" as in democratic regimes "is a new creation that confers sacred status on democratic institutions and symbols."* And in their influential writings, Edward Gibbon and Voltaire claimed that the wars of religion in the sixteenth and seventeenth centuries were "the last gasp of medieval barbarism and fanaticism before the darkness was dispelled."* Gibbon and Voltaire believed that after the Reformation divided Christendom along religious grounds, Protestants and Catholics began killing each other for more than a century, demonstrating the inherent danger of "public" religion. The alleged solution was the modern state, in which religious loyalties were upended and the state secured a monopoly of violence. Henceforth, religious fanaticism would be tamed, uniting all in loyalty to the secular state. However, this is an unfounded "myth of religious violence." The link between state building and war has been well documented, as the historian Charles Tilly noted, "War made the state, and the state made war."* In the actual period of European state building, the most serious cause of violence and the central factor in the growth of the state was the attempt to collect taxes from an unwilling populace with local elites resisting the state-building efforts of kings and emperors. The point is that the rise of the modern state was in no way the solution to the violence of religion. On the contrary, the absorption of church into state that began well before the Reformation was crucial to the rise of the state *and* the wars of the sixteenth and seventeenth centuries.

Nevertheless, Voltaire distinguished between "state religion" and "theological religion" of which "A state religion can never cause any turmoil. This is not true of theological religion; it is the source of all the follies and turmoils imaginable; it is the mother of fanaticism and civil discord; it is the enemy of mankind."* What Rousseau proposed instead was to supplement the purely "private" religion of man with a civil or political religion intended to bind the citizen to the state: "As for that man who, having committed himself publicly to the state's articles of faith, acts on any occasion as if he does not believe them, let his punishment be death. He has committed the greatest of all crimes: he has lied in the presence of the laws."*

Part 2

During the Enlightenment, nationalism became the new civic religion, in which the nation state was not merely a substitute for the church, but a substitute for God, and political religion benefited from being more tangible than supernatural religion in having the physical means of violence necessary to enforce mandatory worship and funding. Nation states provided a new kind of salvation and immortality; one's death is not in vain if it is "for the nation," which will live on.*

This "myth of religious violence" lived on with legal theorist John Rawls who claimed that the modern problem is a theological one and the solution is political. For Rawls, since people believe in unresolvable theological doctrines over which they will kill each other, a secular state must rule.* Similarly, Stanford law professor Kathleen Sullivan, a secularist, has claimed that as a necessary condition for peace to avoid a "war of all sects against all," religion must be banished from the public square.*

As Canavaugh notes, "[O]nce the state had laid claim to the holy, the state voluntarily relinquished it by banning religion from direct access to the public square... then what we have is not a separation of religion from politics but rather the substitution of the religion of the state for the religion of the church."*

Hence, in *Abington Township School District v. Schempp*, Supreme Court Justice William Brennan stated that the function of public schools is:

"the training of American citizens in an atmosphere in which children may assimilate a heritage common to all American groups and religions... This is a heritage neither theistic nor atheistic, but simply civic and patriotic. A patriotic and united allegiance to the United States is the cure for the divisiveness of religion in public."*

In his dissent, Justice Potter Stewart correctly warned that the *Abington* ruling would be seen "not as the realization of state neutrality, but rather as the establishment of a religion of secularism."*

The reality of today's secular theocracy is its hypocritical authoritarianism that circumvents the natural-law tradition of Christian teachings. Cavanaugh well sums up the incoherence of the secular theocrat who claims that, *"Their* violence – being tainted by religion – is uncontrolled, absolutist, fanatical, irrational, and divisive. *Our* violence – being secular – is controlled, modest, rational, beneficial, peace making, and sometimes regrettably necessary to contain their violence."* The appalling problem with the "myth of religious violence" is not that it opposes certain forms of violence, but that it not only denies moral condemnation of *secular* violence but that it considers it highly praiseworthy.*

In *Politics as Religion*, Emilio Gentile notes that the "religion of politics" is "a system of beliefs, myths, rituals, and symbols that interpret and define the meaning and end of human existence by subordinating the destiny of individuals and the collectivity to a supreme entity." A religion of politics is a secular religion because it creates "an aura of sacredness around an entity belonging to this world."* And according to Cavanaugh, "People are not allowed to kill for 'sectarian religion'... Only the nation-state may kill... it is this power to organize killing that makes American civil religion the true religion of the U.S. social order."*

Among most Christians in the U.S. for example, very few would agree to kill in Christ's name, while killing and dying for the nation state in war and supporting "our troops" is taken for granted. The religious-secular split enables public loyalty by Christians to the nation state's secular violence, including invasive wars, torture, and "collateral damage," while avoiding direct confrontation with Christian beliefs about the supremacy of God and natural law teachings.*

Hence, the secular theocracy exalts a sovereign and powerful state that pervades all of life and compels obedience not just to its mandates but to the secular nationalism of the Zeitgeist itself, for which the populace is forced to conform to and fund. This worldview dominates public schools, colleges and universities, elite media, entertainment, and an ever-expanding array of government domains in law, health care, welfare, retirement, transportation, commerce, parks and recreation, etc. Not coincidentally in the modern era when nation states have displaced God, Cavanaugh notes, "it does not matter that the U.S. flag does not explicitly refer to a god. It is nevertheless a sacred – perhaps the most sacred – object in U.S. society and is thus an object of religious veneration."* And worship in the secular theocracy in schools and at public events consists of singing the "National Anthem" and saluting the flag in "The Pledge of Allegiance," which as described by its socialist author Francis Bellamy, "is the same with the catechism, or the Lord's Prayer."*

In contrast, C.S. Lewis understood that natural law applies to *all* human behavior including government officials, and he clearly saw that government power was a dangerous force that needs to be strictly limited.* Contrary to secular interpretations of the Establishment Clause, the issue is not "the separation of church and state" into distinct and conflicting realms but the *reduction* of state power to micro-minute levels in order to eliminate the establishment of a state-backed church of any kind. Individuals have property rights that are sacred and need to be protected under a uniform rule of law, Christianity instructs us in the civic virtues upon which such law depends, and good ends can only be pursued using good means. The result is the recognition that compelling people into some collectivist regimentation is evil and produces immense human suffering. Lewis noted that:

> "I do not like the pretensions of Government – the grounds on which it demands my obedience – to be pitched too high. I don't like

the medicine-man's magical pretensions nor the Bourbon's Divine Right. This is not solely because I disbelieve in magic and in Bossuet's *Politique*. I believe in God, but I detest theocracy. For every Government consists of mere men and is, strictly viewed, a makeshift; if it adds to its commands 'Thus saith the Lord,' it lies, and lies dangerously."*

The point is that the natural law is rooted in the *religio* of Christianity and sets the epistemic and moral foundation and context for the existence of all people as individuals and that such laws make the cooperation, norms, and relationships of community possible. To break the natural law in the name of a secular theocracy is to simultaneously break the relational bonds of community that are the basis for the natural rights of all individuals to be free and responsible.

Moreover, the solution is to end secular theocracy by de-socializing the public square, not seek to "take over" this theocracy. This means privatizing government schools, transportation, welfare, retirement, parks and recreation, commerce, civic areas of all types, etc., and allowing covenants and other private institutions and communities to flourish.* Those who believe that such government domains are workable and should be exempt from natural law tenets are hubristically fooling themselves and end up embracing the moral relativism of utilitarianism. As Lewis further noted:

"[S]ince we have sin, we have found, as Lord Acton says, that 'all power corrupts, and absolute power corrupts absolutely.' The only remedy has been to take away the powers... Theocracy has been rightly abolished not because it is bad that priests should govern ignorant laymen, but because priests are wicked men like the rest of us."*

Section Three – Economy

11

I, Pencil

by Leonard E. Read

I am a lead pencil – the ordinary wooden pencil familiar to all boys and girls and adults who can read and write. Writing is both my vocation and my avocation; that's all I do.

You may wonder why I should write a genealogy. Well, to begin with, my story is interesting. And, next, I am a mystery – more so than a tree or a sunset or even a flash of lightning. But, sadly, I am taken for granted by those who use me, as if I were a mere incident and without background. This supercilious attitude relegates me to the level of the commonplace. This is a species of the grievous error in which mankind cannot too long persist without peril. For, the wise G. K. Chesterton observed, "We are perishing for want of wonder, not for want of wonders."

I, Pencil, simple though I appear to be, merit your wonder and awe, a claim I shall attempt to prove. In fact, if you can understand me – no, that's too much to ask of anyone – if you can become aware of the miraculousness which I symbolize, you can help save the freedom mankind is so unhappily losing. I have a profound lesson to teach. And I can teach this lesson better than can an automobile or an airplane or a mechanical dishwasher because – well, because I am seemingly so simple. Simple? Yet, *not a single person on the face of this earth knows how to make me.* This sounds fantastic, doesn't it? Especially when it is realized that there are about one and one-half billion of my kind produced in the U.S.A. each year.

Pick me up and look me over. What do you see? Not much meets the eye – there's some wood, lacquer, the printed labeling, graphite lead, a bit of metal, and an eraser.

Innumerable Antecedents

Just as you cannot trace your family tree back very far, so is it impossible for me to name and explain all my antecedents. But I would like to suggest enough of them to impress upon you the richness and complexity of my background.

My family tree begins with what in fact is a tree, a cedar of straight grain that grows in Northern California and Oregon. Now contemplate all the saws and trucks and rope and the countless other gear used in harvesting and carting the cedar logs to the railroad siding. Think of all the persons and the numberless skills that went into their fabrication: the mining of ore, the making of steel and its refinement into saws, axes, motors; the growing of hemp and bringing it through all the stages to heavy and strong rope; the logging camps with their beds and mess halls, the cookery and the raising of all the foods. Why, untold thousands of persons had a hand in every cup of coffee the loggers drink!

The logs are shipped to a mill in San Leandro, California. Can you imagine the individuals who make flat cars and rails and railroad engines and who construct and install the communication systems incidental thereto? These legions are among my antecedents.

Consider the millwork in San Leandro. The cedar logs are cut into small, pencil-length slats less than one-fourth of an inch in thickness. These are kiln dried and then tinted for the same reason women put rouge on their faces. People prefer that I look pretty, not a pallid white. The slats are waxed and kiln dried again. How many skills went into the making of the tint and the kilns, into supplying the heat, the light and power, the belts, motors, and all the other things a mill requires? Sweepers in the mill among my ancestors? Yes, and included are the men who poured the concrete for the dam of a Pacific Gas & Electric Company hydroplant which supplies the mill's power!

Don't overlook the ancestors present and distant who have a hand in transporting sixty carloads of slats across the nation.

Once in the pencil factory – $4,000,000 in machinery and building, all capital accumulated by thrifty and saving parents of mine – each slat is given eight grooves by a complex machine, after which another machine lays leads in every other slat, applies glue, and places another slat atop – a lead sandwich, so to speak. Seven brothers and I are mechanically carved from this "wood-clinched" sandwich.

My "lead" itself – it contains no lead at all – is complex. The graphite is mined in Ceylon. Consider these miners and those who make their many tools and the makers of the paper sacks in which the graphite is shipped and those who make the string that ties the sacks and those who put them aboard ships and those who make the ships. Even the lighthouse keepers along the way assisted in my birth – and the harbor pilots.

The graphite is mixed with clay from Mississippi in which ammonium hydroxide is used in the refining process. Then wetting agents are added such as sulfonated tallow – animal fats chemically reacted with sulfuric acid. After passing through numerous machines, the mixture finally appears as endless extrusions – as from a sausage grinder – cut to size, dried, and baked for several hours at 1,850 degrees Fahrenheit. To increase their strength and smoothness the leads are then treated with a hot mixture which includes candelilla wax from Mexico, paraffin wax, and hydrogenated natural fats.

My cedar receives six coats of lacquer. Do you know all the ingredients of lacquer? Who would think that the growers of castor beans and the refiners of castor oil are a part of it? They are. Why, even the processes by which the lacquer is made a beautiful yellow involves the skills of more persons than one can enumerate!

Observe the labeling. That's a film formed by applying heat to carbon black mixed with resins. How do you make resins and what, pray, is carbon black?

My bit of metal – the ferrule – is brass. Think of all the persons who mine zinc and copper and those who have the skills to make shiny sheet brass from these products of nature. Those black rings on my ferrule are black nickel. What is black nickel and how is it applied? The complete story of why the center of my ferrule has no black nickel on it would take pages to explain.

Then there's my crowning glory, inelegantly referred to in the trade as "the plug," the part man uses to erase the errors he makes with me. An ingredient called "factice" is what does the erasing. It is a rubber-like product made by reacting rape-seed oil from the Dutch East Indies with sulfur chloride. Rubber, contrary to the common notion, is only for binding purposes. Then, too, there are numerous vulcanizing and accelerating agents. The pumice comes from Italy; and the pigment which gives "the plug" its color is cadmium sulfide.

No One Knows

Does anyone wish to challenge my earlier assertion that no single person on the face of this earth knows how to make me?

Actually, millions of human beings have had a hand in my creation, no one of whom even knows more than a very few of the others. Now, you may say that I go too far in relating the picker of a coffee berry in far off Brazil and food growers elsewhere to my creation; that this is an extreme position. I shall stand by my claim. There isn't a single person in all these millions, including the president of the pencil company, who contributes more than a tiny, infinitesimal bit of know-how. From the standpoint of know-how the only difference between the miner of graphite in Ceylon and the logger in Oregon is in the *type* of know-how. Neither the miner nor the logger can be dispensed with, any more than can the chemist at the factory or the worker in the oil field – paraffin being a by-product of petroleum.

Here is an astounding fact: *Neither* the worker in the oil field nor the chemist nor the digger of graphite or clay nor any who mans or makes the ships or trains or trucks nor the one who runs the machine that does the knurling on my bit of metal nor the president of the company performs his singular task because he wants me. Each one wants me less, perhaps, than does a child in the first grade. Indeed, there are some among this vast multitude who never saw a pencil nor would they know how to use one. Their motivation is other than me. Perhaps it is something like this: Each of these millions sees that he can thus exchange his tiny know-how for the goods and services he needs or wants. I may or may not be among these items.

No Master Mind

There is a fact still more astounding: the absence of a master mind, of anyone dictating or forcibly directing these countless actions which bring me into being. No trace of such a person can be found. Instead, we find the Invisible Hand at work. This is the mystery to which I earlier referred.

It has been said that "only God can make a tree." Why do we agree with this? Isn't it because we realize that we ourselves could not make one? Indeed, can we even describe a tree? We cannot, except in superficial terms. We can say, for instance, that a certain molecular configuration manifests itself as a tree. But what mind is there among men that could even record, let alone direct, the constant changes in molecules that transpire in the life span of a tree? Such a feat is utterly unthinkable!

I, Pencil, am a complex combination of miracles: a tree, zinc, copper, graphite, and so on. But to these miracles which manifest themselves in Nature an even more extraordinary miracle has been added: the configuration of creative human energies – millions of tiny know-hows configurating naturally and spontaneously in response to human necessity and desire and *in the absence of any human master-minding!* Since only God can make a tree, I insist that only God could make me. Man can no more direct these millions of know-hows to bring me into being than he can put molecules together to create a tree.

The above is what I meant when writing, "If you can become aware of the miraculousness which I symbolize, you can help save the freedom mankind is so unhappily losing." For, if one is aware that these know-hows will naturally, yes, automatically, arrange themselves into creative and productive patterns in response to human necessity and demand – that is, in the absence of governmental or any other coercive master-minding – then one will possess an absolutely essential ingredient for freedom: *a faith in free people*. Freedom is impossible without this faith.

Once government has had a monopoly of a creative activity such, for instance, as the delivery of the mails, most individuals will believe that the mails could not be efficiently delivered by men acting freely. And here is the reason: Each one acknowledges that he himself doesn't know how to do all the things incident to mail delivery. He also recognizes that no other individual could do it. These assumptions are correct. No individual possesses enough know-how to perform a nation's mail delivery any more than any individual possesses enough know-how to make a pencil. Now, in the absence of faith in free people – in the unawareness that millions of tiny know-hows would naturally and miraculously form and cooperate to satisfy this necessity – the individual cannot help but reach the erroneous conclusion that mail can be delivered only by governmental "master-minding."

Testimony Galore

If I, Pencil, were the only item that could offer testimony on what men and women can accomplish when free to try, then those with little faith would have a fair case. However, there is testimony galore; it's all about us and on every hand. Mail delivery is exceedingly simple when compared, for instance, to the making of an automobile or a calculating machine or a grain combine or a milling machine or to tens of thousands of other things. Delivery? Why, in this area where men have been left free to try, they deliver the human voice around the world in less than one second; they deliver an event visually and in motion to any person's home when it is happening; they deliver 150 passengers from Seattle to Baltimore in less than four hours; they deliver gas from Texas to one's range or furnace in New York at unbelievably low rates and without subsidy; they deliver each four pounds of oil from the Persian Gulf to our Eastern Seaboard – halfway around the world – for less money than the government charges for delivering a one-ounce letter across the street!

The lesson I have to teach is this: *Leave all creative energies uninhibited.* Merely organize society to act in harmony with this lesson. Let society's legal apparatus remove all obstacles the best it can. Permit these creative know-hows freely to flow. Have faith that free men and women will respond to the Invisible Hand. This faith will be confirmed. I, Pencil, seemingly simple though I am, offer the miracle of my creation as testimony that this is a practical faith, as practical as the sun, the rain, a cedar tree, and the good earth.

12
What is the Free Market?
by Murray N. Rothbard

The Free Market is a summary term for an array of exchanges that take place in society. Each exchange is undertaken as a voluntary agreement between two people or between groups of people represented by agents. These two individuals (or agents) exchange two economic goods, either tangible commodities or nontangible services. Thus, when I buy a newspaper from a news dealer for fifty cents, the news dealer and I exchange two commodities: I give up fifty cents, and the news dealer gives up the newspaper. Or if I work for a corporation, I exchange my labor services, in a mutually agreed way, for a monetary salary; here the corporation is represented by a manager (an agent) with the authority to hire.

Both parties undertake the exchange because each expects to gain from it. Also, each will repeat the exchange next time (or refuse to) because his expectation has proved correct (or incorrect) in the recent past. Trade, or exchange, is engaged in precisely because both parties benefit; if they did not expect to gain, they would not agree to the exchange.

This simple reasoning refutes the argument against free trade typical of the "mercantilist" period of sixteenth- to eighteenth-century Europe, and classically expounded by the famed sixteenth-century French essayist Montaigne. The mercantilists argued that in any trade, one party can benefit only at the expense of the other, that in every transaction there is a winner and a loser, an "exploiter" and an "exploited." We can immediately see the fallacy in this still-popular viewpoint: the willingness and even eagerness to trade means that both parties benefit. In modern game-theory jargon, trade is a win-win situation, a "positive-sum" rather than a "zero-sum" or "negative-sum" game.

How can both parties benefit from an exchange? Each one values the two goods or services differently, and these differences set the scene for an exchange. I, for example, am walking along with money in my pocket but no newspaper; the news dealer, on the other hand, has plenty of newspapers but is anxious to acquire money. And so, finding each other, we strike a deal.

Two factors determine the terms of any agreement: how much each participant values each good in question, and each participant's bargaining skills. How many cents will exchange for one newspaper, or how many Mickey Mantle baseball cards will swap for a Babe Ruth, depends on all the participants in the newspaper market or the baseball card market – on how much each one values the cards as compared to the other goods he could buy. These terms of exchange, called "prices" (of newspapers in terms of money, or of Babe Ruth cards in terms of Mickey Mantles), are ultimately determined by how many newspapers, or baseball cards, are available on the market in relation to how favorably buyers evaluate these goods. In short, by the interaction of their supply with the demand for them.

Given the supply of a good, an increase in its value in the minds of the buyers will raise the demand for the good, more money will be bid for it, and its price will rise. The reverse occurs if the value, and therefore the demand, for the good falls. On the other hand, given the buyers' evaluation, or demand for a good, if the supply increases, each unit of supply – each baseball card or loaf of bread – will fall in value, and therefore, the price of the good will fall. The reverse occurs if the supply of the good decreases.

The market, then, is not simply an array, but a highly complex, interacting latticework of exchanges. In primitive societies, exchanges are all barter or direct exchange. Two people trade two directly useful goods, such as horses for cows or Mickey Mantles for Babe Ruths. But as a society develops, a step-by-step process of mutual benefit creates a situation in which one or two broadly useful and valuable commodities are chosen on the market as a medium of indirect exchange. This money-commodity, generally but not always gold or silver, is then demanded not only for its own sake, but even more to facilitate a re-exchange for another desired commodity. It is much easier to pay steelworkers not in steel bars, but in money, with which the workers can then buy whatever they desire. They are willing to accept money because they know from experience and insight that everyone else in the society will also accept that money in payment.

The modern, almost infinite latticework of exchanges, the market, is made possible by the use of money. Each person engages in specialization, or a division of labor, producing what he or she is best at. Production begins with natural resources, and then various forms of machines and capital goods, until finally, goods are sold to the consumer. At each stage of production from natural resource to consumer good, money is voluntarily exchanged for capital goods, labor services, and land resources. At each step of the way, terms of exchanges, or prices, are determined by the voluntary interactions of suppliers and demanders. This market is "free" because choices, at each step, are made freely and voluntarily.

The free market and the free price system make goods from around the world available to consumers. The free market also gives the largest possible scope to entrepreneurs, who risk capital to allocate resources so as to satisfy the future desires of the mass of consumers as efficiently as possible. Saving and investment can then develop capital goods and increase the productivity and wages of workers, thereby increasing their standard of living. The free competitive market also rewards and stimulates technological innovation that allows the innovator to get a head start in satisfying consumer wants in new and creative ways.

Not only is investment encouraged, but perhaps more important, the price system, and the profit-and-loss incentives of the market, guide capital investment and production into the proper paths. The intricate latticework can mesh and "clear" all markets so that there are no sudden, unforeseen, and inexplicable shortages and surpluses anywhere in the production system.

But exchanges are not necessarily free. Many are coerced. If a robber threatens you with "Your money or your life," your payment to him is coerced and not voluntary, and he benefits at your expense. It is robbery, not free markets, that actually follows the mercantilist model: the robber benefits at the expense of the coerced. Exploitation occurs not in the free market, but where the coercer exploits his victim. In the long run, coercion is a negative-sum game that leads to reduced production, saving, and investment, a depleted stock of capital, and reduced productivity and living standards for all, perhaps even for the coercers themselves.

Government, in every society, is the only lawful system of coercion. Taxation is a coerced exchange, and the heavier the burden of taxation on production, the more likely it is that economic growth will falter and decline. Other forms of government coercion (e.g., price controls or restrictions that prevent new competitors from entering a market) hamper and cripple market exchanges, while others (prohibitions on deceptive practices, enforcement of contracts) can facilitate voluntary exchanges.

The ultimate in government coercion is socialism. Under socialist central planning the socialist planning board lacks a price system for land or capital goods. As even socialists like Robert Heilbroner now admit, the socialist planning board therefore has no way to calculate prices or costs or to invest capital so that the latticework of production meshes and clears. The current Soviet experience, where a bumper wheat harvest somehow cannot find its way to retail stores, is an instructive example of the impossibility of operating a complex, modern economy in the absence of a free market. There was neither incentive nor means of calculating prices and costs for hopper cars to get to the wheat, for the flour mills to receive and process it, and so on down through the large number of stages needed to reach the ultimate consumer in Moscow or Sverdlovsk. The investment in wheat is almost totally wasted.

Market socialism is, in fact, a contradiction in terms. The fashionable discussion of market socialism often overlooks one crucial aspect of the market. When two goods are indeed exchanged, what is really exchanged is the property titles in those goods. When I buy a newspaper for fifty cents, the seller and I are exchanging property titles: I yield the ownership of the fifty cents and grant it to the news dealer, and he yields the ownership of the newspaper to me. The exact same process occurs as in buying a house, except that in the case of the newspaper, matters are much more informal, and we can all avoid the intricate process of deeds, notarized contracts, agents, attorneys, mortgage brokers, and so on. But the economic nature of the two transactions remains the same.

This means that the key to the existence and flourishing of the free market is a society in which the rights and titles of private property are respected, defended, and kept secure. The key to socialism, on the other hand, is government ownership of the means of production, land, and capital goods. Thus, there can be no market in land or capital goods worthy of the name.

Some critics of the free-market argue that property rights are in conflict with "human" rights. But the critics fail to realize that in a free-market system, every person has a property right over his own person and his own labor, and that he can make free contracts for those services. Slavery violates the basic property right of the slave over his own body and person, a right that is the groundwork for any person's property rights over non-human material objects. What's more, all rights are human rights, whether it is everyone's right to free speech or one individual's property rights in his own home.

A common charge against the free-market society is that it institutes "the law of the jungle," of "dog eat dog," that it spurns human cooperation for competition, and that it exalts material success as opposed to spiritual values, philosophy, or leisure activities. On the contrary, the jungle is precisely a society of coercion, theft, and parasitism, a society that demolishes lives and living standards. The peaceful market competition of producers and suppliers is a profoundly cooperative process in which everyone benefits, and where everyone's living standard flourishes (compared to what it would be in an unfree society). And the undoubted material success of free societies provides the general affluence that permits us to enjoy an enormous amount of leisure as compared to other societies, and to pursue matters of the spirit. It is the coercive countries with little or no market activity, notably under communism, where the grind of daily existence not only impoverishes people materially, but deadens their spirit.

13
Planning vs. the Free Market
by Henry Hazlitt

When we discuss "economic planning," we must be clear concerning what it is we are talking about. The real question being raised is not: plan or no plan? but *whose* plan?

Each of us, in his private capacity, is constantly planning for the future: what he will do the rest of today, the rest of the week, or on the weekend; what he will do this month or next year. Some of us are planning, though in a more general way, ten or twenty years ahead.

We are making these plans both in our capacity as consumers and as producers. Employees are either planning to stay where they are, or to shift from one job to another, or from one company to another, or from one city to another, or even from one career to another. Entrepreneurs are either planning to stay in one location or to move to another, to expand or contract their operations, to stop making a product for which they think demand is dying and to start making one for which they think demand is going to grow.

Now the people who call themselves "Economic Planners" either ignore or by implication deny all this. They talk as if the world of private enterprise, the free market, supply, demand, and competition, were a world of chaos and anarchy, in which nobody ever planned ahead or looked ahead, but merely drifted or staggered along. I once engaged in a television debate with an eminent Planner in a high official position who implied that without his forecasts and guidance American business would be "flying blind." At best, the Planners imply, the world of private enterprise is one in which everybody works or plans at cross purposes or makes his plans solely in his "private" interest rather than in the "public" interest.

Now the Planner wants to substitute his own plan for the plans of everybody else. At best, he wants the *government* to lay down a Master Plan to which everybody else's plan must be subordinated.

It Involves Compulsion

It is this aspect of Planning to which our attention should be directed: Planning always involves *compulsion*. This may be disguised in various ways. The government Planners will, of course, try to persuade people that the Master Plan has been drawn up for their own good, and that the only persons who are going to be coerced are those whose plans are "not in the public interest."

The Planners will say, in the newly fashionable phraseology, that their plans are not "imperative," but merely "indicative." They will make a great parade of "democracy," freedom, cooperation, and noncompulsion by "consulting all groups" – "Labor," "Industry," the Government, even "Consumers Representatives" – in drawing up the Master Plan and the specific "goals" or "targets." Of course, if they could really succeed in giving everybody his proportionate weight and voice and freedom of choice, if everybody were allowed to pursue the plan of production or consumption of specific goods and services that he had intended to pursue or would have pursued anyway, then the whole Plan would be useless and pointless, a complete waste of energy and time. The Plan would be meaningful only if it forced the production and consumption of *different* things or different quantities of things than a free market would have provided. In short, it would be meaningful only insofar as it put compulsion on *somebody* and forced some change in the pattern of production and consumption.

There are two excuses for this coercion. One is that the free market produces the *wrong* goods, and that only government Planning and direction could assure the production of the "right" ones. This is the thesis popularized by J. K. Galbraith. The other excuse is that the free market does not produce *enough* goods, and that only government Planning could speed things up. This is the thesis of the apostles of "economic growth."

The "Five-Year Plans"

Let us take up the "Galbraith" thesis first. I put his name in quotation marks because the thesis long antedates his presentation of it. It is the basis of all the communist "Five-Year Plans" which are now aped by a score of socialist nations. While these Plans may consist in setting out some general "overall" percentage of production increase, their characteristic feature is rather a whole network of specific "targets" for specific industries: there is to be a 25 percent increase in steel capacity, a 15 percent increase in cement production, a 12 percent increase in butter and milk output, and so forth.

There is always a strong bias in these Plans, especially in the communist countries, in favor of heavy industry, because it gives increased power to make war. In all the Plans, however, even in noncommunist countries, there is a strong bias in favor of industrialization, of heavy industry as against agriculture, in the belief that this necessarily increases real income faster and leads to greater national self-sufficiency. It is not an accident that such countries are constantly running into agricultural crises and food famines.

But the Plans also reflect either the implied or explicit moral judgments of the government Planners. The latter seldom plan for an increased production of cigarettes or whisky, or, in fact, for any so-called "luxury" item. The standards are always grim and puritanical. The word "austerity" makes a chronic appearance. Consumers are told that they must "tighten their belts" for a little longer. Sometimes, if the last Plan has not been too unsuccessful, there is a little relaxation: consumers can, perhaps, have a few more motor cars and hospitals and playgrounds. But there is almost never any provision for, say, more golf courses or even bowling alleys. In general, no form of expenditure is approved that cannot be universalized, or at least "majoritized." And such so-called luxury expenditure is discouraged, even in a so-called "indicative" Plan, by not allowing access by promoters of such projects to bank credit or to the capital markets. At some point government coercion or compulsion comes into play.

Austerity Leads to Waste

This disapproval and coercion may rest on several grounds. Nearly all "austerity" programs stem from the belief, not that the person who wants to make a "luxury" expenditure cannot afford it, but that "the nation" cannot afford it. This involves the assumption that, if I set up a bowling alley or patronize one, I am somehow depriving my fellow citizens of more necessary goods or services. This would be true only on the assumption that the proper thing to do is to tax my so-called surplus income away from me and turn it over to others in the form of money, goods, or services. But if I am allowed to keep my "surplus" income, and am forbidden to spend it on bowling alleys or on imported wine and cheese, I will spend it on something else that is not forbidden. Thus when the British austerity program after World War II prevented an Englishman from consuming imported luxuries, on the ground that "the nation" could not afford the "foreign exchange" or the "unfavorable balance of payments," officials were shocked to find that the money was being squandered on football pools or dog races. And there is no reason to suppose, in any case, that the "dollar shortage" or the "unfavorable balance of payments" was helped in the least. The austerity program, insofar as it was not enforced by higher income taxes, probably cut down potential exports as much as it did potential imports;

and insofar as it was enforced by higher income taxes, it discouraged exports by restricting and discouraging production.

Bureaucratic Choice

But we come now to the specific Galbraith thesis, growing out of the agelong bureaucratic suspicion of luxury spending, that consumers generally do not know how to spend the income they have earned; that they buy whatever advertisers tell them to buy; that consumers are, in short, boobs and suckers, chronically wasting their money on trivialities, if not on absolute junk. The bulk of consumers also, if left to themselves, show atrocious taste, and crave cerise automobiles with ridiculous tailfins.

The natural conclusion from all this – and Galbraith does not hesitate to draw it – is that consumers ought to be deprived of freedom of choice, and that government bureaucrats, full of wisdom – of course, of a very unconventional wisdom – should make their consumptive choices for them. The consumers should be supplied, not with what they themselves want, but with what bureaucrats of exquisite taste and culture think is good for them. And the way to do this is to tax away from people all the income they have been foolish enough to earn above that required to meet their bare necessities, and turn it over to the bureaucrats to be spent in ways in which the latter think would really do people the most good – more and better roads and parks and play grounds and schools and television programs – all supplied, of course, by government.

And here Galbraith resorts to a neat semantic trick. The goods and services for which people voluntarily spend their own money make up, in his vocabulary, the "private sector" of the economy, while the goods and services supplied to them by the government, out of the income it has seized from them in taxes, make up the "public sector." Now the adjective "private" carries an aura of the selfish and exclusive, the inward-looking, whereas the adjective "public" carries an aura of the democratic, the shared, the generous, the patriotic, the outward-looking – in brief, the public-spirited. And as the tendency of the expanding welfare state has been, in fact, to take out of private hands and more and more take into its own hands provision of the goods and services that are considered to be most essential and most edifying – roads and water supply, schools and hospitals and scientific research, education, old-age insurance and medical care – the tendency must be increasingly to associate the word "public" with everything that is really necessary and laudable, leaving the "private sector" to be associated merely with the superfluities and capricious wants that are left over after everything that is really important has been taken care of.

If the distinction between the two "sectors" were put in more neutral terms – say, the "private sector" versus the "governmental sector," the scales would not be so heavily weighted in favor of the latter. In fact, this more neutral vocabulary would raise in the mind of the hearer the question whether certain activities now assumed by the modern welfare state do legitimately or appropriately come within the governmental province. For Galbraith's use of the word "sector," "private" or "public," cleverly carries the implication that the public "sector" is legitimately not only whatever the government has already taken over but a great deal besides. Galbraith's whole point is that the "public sector" is "starved" in favor of a "private sector" overstuffed with superfluities and trash.

The Voluntary Way

The true distinction, and the appropriate vocabulary, however, would throw an entirely different light on the matter. What Galbraith calls the "private sector" of the economy is, in fact, the *voluntary* sector; and what he calls the "public sector" is, in fact, the *coercive* sector. The voluntary sector is made up of the goods and services for which people voluntarily spend the money they have earned. The coercive sector is made up of the goods and services that are provided, regardless of the wishes of the in-dividual, out of the taxes that are seized from him. And as this sector grows at the expense of the voluntary sector, we come to the essence of the wel-fare state. In this state nobody pays for the education of his own children but everybody pays for the education of everybody else's children. Nobody pays his own medical bills, but everybody pays everybody else's medical bills. Nobody helps his own old parents, but everybody else's old parents. Nobody provides for the contingency of his own unemployment, his own sickness, his own old age, but everybody provides for the unemployment, sickness, or old age of everybody else. The welfare state, as Bastiat put it with uncanny clairvoyance more than a century ago, is the great fiction by which everybody tries to live at the expense of everybody else.

This is not only a fiction; it is bound to be a failure. This is sure to be the outcome whenever effort is separated from reward. When people who earn more than the average have their "surplus," or the greater part of it, seized from them in taxes, and when people who earn less than the average have the deficiency, or the greater part of it, turned over to them in hand-outs and doles, the production of all must sharply decline; for the energetic and able lose their incentive to produce more than the average, and the slothful and unskilled lose their incentive to improve their condition.

The Growth Planners

I have spent so much time in analyzing the fallacies of the Galbraithian school of economic Planners that I have left myself little in which to analyze the fallacies of the Growth Planners. Many of their fallacies are the same; but there are some important differences.

The chief difference is that the Galbraithians believe that a free market economy produces too much (though, of course, they are the "wrong" goods), whereas the Growthmen believe that a free market economy does not produce nearly enough. I will not here deal with all the statistical errors, gaps, and fallacies in their arguments, though an analysis of these alone could occupy a fat book. I want to concentrate on their idea that some form of government direction or coercion can by some strange magic increase production above the level that can be achieved when everybody enjoys economic freedom.

For it seems to me self-evident that when people are free, production tends to be, if not maximized, at least optimized. This is because, in a system of free markets and private property, everybody's reward tends to equal the value of his production. What he gets for his production (and is allowed to keep) is in fact what it is worth in the market. If he wants to double his income in a single year, he is free to try – and may succeed if he is able to double his production in a single year. If he is content with the income he has – or if he feels that he can only get more by excessive effort or risk – he is under no pressure to increase his output. In a free market everyone is free to maximize his satisfactions, whether these consist in more leisure or in more goods.

But along comes the Growth Planner. He finds by statistics (whose trustworthiness and accuracy he never doubts) that the economy has been growing, say, only 2.8 percent a year. He concludes, in a flash of genius, that a growth rate of 5 percent a year would be faster!

There is among the Growth Planners a profound mystical belief in the power of words. They declare that they "are not satisfied" with a growth rate of a mere 2.8 percent a year; they demand a growth rate of 5 percent a year. And once having spoken, they act as if half the job had already been done. If they did not assume this, it would be impossible to explain the deep earnestness with which they argue among themselves whether the growth rate "ought" to be 4 or 5 or 6 percent. (The only thing they always agree on is that it ought to be greater than whatever it actually is.) Having decided on this magic overall figure, they then proceed either to set specific targets for specific goods (and here they are at one with the Russian Five-Year Planners) or to announce some general recipe for reaching the overall rate.

But why do they assume that setting their magic target rate will increase the rate of production over the existing one? And how is their growth rate supposed to apply as far as the individual is concerned? Is the man who is already making $50,000 a year to be coerced into working for an income of $52,500 next year? Is the man who is making only $5,000 a year to be forbidden to make more than $5,250 next year? If not, what is gained by making a specific "annual growth rate" a governmental "target"? Why not just permit or encourage everybody to do his best, or make his own decision, and let the average "growth" be whatever it turns out to be?

The way to get a maximum rate of "economic growth" – assuming this to be our aim – is to give maximum encouragement to production, employment, saving, and investment. And the way to do this is to maintain a free market and a sound currency. It is to encourage profits, which must in turn encourage both investment and employment. It is to refrain from oppressive taxation that siphons away the funds that would otherwise be available for investment. It is to allow free wage rates that permit and encourage full employment. It is to allow free interest rates, which would tend to maximize saving and investment.

The Wrong Policies

The way to *slow down* the rate of economic growth is, of course, precisely the opposite of this. It is to discourage production, employment, saving, and investment by incessant interventions, controls, threats, and harassment. It is to frown upon profits, to declare that they are excessive, to file constant antitrust suits, to control prices by law or by threats, to levy confiscatory taxes that discourage new investment and siphon off the funds that make investment possible, to hold down interest rates artificially to the point where real saving is discouraged and malinvestment encouraged, to deprive employers of genuine freedom of bargaining, to grant excessive immunities and privileges to labor unions so that their demands are chronically excessive and chronically threaten unemployment – and then to try to offset all these policies by government spending, deficits, and monetary inflation. But I have just described precisely the policies that most of the fanatical Growth-men advocate.

Their recipe for inducing growth always turns out to be – inflation. This does lead to the *illusion* of growth, which is measured in their statistics in monetary terms. What the Growthmen do not realize is that the magic of inflation is always a short-run magic, and quickly played out. It can work temporarily and under special conditions – when it causes prices to rise faster than wages and so restores or expands profit margins. But this can happen only in the early stages of an inflation which is not expected to continue. And it can happen even then only because of the temporary acquiescence or passivity of the labor union leaders. The consequences of this short-lived paradise are malinvestment, waste, a wanton redistribution of wealth and income, the growth of speculation and gambling, immorality and corruption, social resentment, discontent and upheaval, disillusion, bankruptcy, increased governmental controls, and eventual collapse. This year's euphoria becomes next year's hangover. Sound long-run growth is always retarded.

In Spite of "The Plan"

Before closing, I should like to deal with at least one statistical argument in favor of government Planning. This is that Planning has actually succeeded in promoting growth, and that this can be statistically proved. In reply I should like to quote from an article on economic planning in the *Survey* published by the Morgan Guaranty Trust Company of New York in its issue of June 1962:

"There is no way to be sure how much credit is due the French plans in themselves for that country's impressive 4½ percent average annual growth rate over the past decade. Other factors were working in favor of growth: a relatively low starting level after the wartime destruction, Marshall Plan funds in the early years, later an ample labor supply siphonable from agriculture and from obsolete or inefficient industries, most recently the bracing air of foreign competition let in by liberalization of import restrictions, the general dynamism of the Common Market, the break-through of the consumer as a source of demand. For the fact that France today has a high degree of stability and a strong currency along with its growth, the stern fiscal discipline applied after the devaluation of late 1958 must be held principally responsible.

"That a plan is fulfilled, in other words, does not prove that the same or better results could not have been achieved with a lesser degree of central guidance. Any judgment as to cause and effect, of course, must also consider the cases of West Germany and Italy, which have sustained high growth rates without national planning of the economy."

In brief, statistical estimates of growth rates, even if we could accept them as meaningful and accurate, are the result of so many factors that it is never possible to ascribe them with confidence to any single cause. Ultimately we must fall back upon an *a priori* conclusion, yet a conclusion that is confirmed by the whole range of human experience: that when each of us is free to work out his own economic destiny, within the framework of the market economy, the institution of private property, and the general rule of law, we will all improve our economic condition much faster than when we are ordered around by bureaucrats.

14
Historical Capitalism
vs. the Free Market
by Richard Ebeling

During the dark days of Nazi collectivism in Europe, the German economist Wilhelm Röpke used the haven of neutral Switzerland for continuing to write and lecture on the moral and economic principles of the free society. "Collectivism," he warned, was "the fundamental and moral danger of the West." The triumph of collectivism meant "nothing less than political and economic tyranny, regimentation, centralization of every department of life, the destruction of personality, totalitarianism and the rigid mechanization of human society."

If the Western world was to be saved, Röpke said, it would require a "renaissance of [classical] Liberalism" springing "from an elementary longing for freedom and for the resuscitation of human individuality." At the same time, such a renaissance was inseparable from the establishing of a capitalist economy. But what is capitalism? "Now here at once we are faced with a difficulty," Röpke lamented, because "capitalism contains so many ambiguities that it is becoming ever less adapted for an honest spiritual currency."

As a solution, Röpke suggested that we "make a sharp distinction between the principle of a market economy as such... and the actual development which during the nineteenth and twentieth centuries has led to the historical foundation of market economy... If the word 'Capitalism' is to be used at all this should be with due reserve and then at most only to designate this historical form of market economy... Only in this way we are safe from the danger... of making the principle of the market economy responsible for things which are to be attributed to the whole historical combination... of economic, social, legal, moral and cultural elements... in which it (capitalism) appeared in the nineteenth century."

Röpke's distinction between the principle of a capitalist or market economy and the historical forms in which capitalism has manifested itself in various times is as important now in the post-Soviet socialist era of the 1990s as when he presented his argument during the zenith of Nazi socialism in the 1940s.

In the face of the collapse of communism as an ideology and as a practical economic system, the market economy is being hailed by some and reluctantly conceded by others to be the only decent and viable economic order. The Eastern European countries declare their desire to construct capitalist economics on the ruins of their socialist past. In increasing parts of Asia and South America, liberalized markets and privatization of state enterprises are said to be among the goals of governmental policy. And in both Western Europe and the United States, all the major political parties insist that they are "pro-market" for purposes of generating economic growth, increased employment and technological innovations.

Capitalism stands triumphant. But what is "capitalism"? The fact is that the market economy has evolved both in Europe and the United States during the last two hundred years in the historical context of the following: conflicting cultures and world views, contradictory political philosophies, special-interest intrigues in the face of economic and institutional changes, and ideological wars both on and off the battlefields of the world.

As a consequence, even before all of the implications and requirements for a free-market economy could be fully appreciated and implemented in the 19th century, it was being opposed and subverted by the residues of feudal privilege and mercantilist ideology. And even as the proponents of the market economy were proclaiming their victory over oppressive and intrusive government in the middle of the 19th century, new forces of collectivist reaction were arising in the form of socialism and communism. Three ideas in particular undermined the principle of the market economy, and, as a result, historical capitalism has contained within it the seeds of its own destruction.

1. *The Idea of the National Interest and the Rationale for "Public Policy."* In the 17th and 18th centuries, the emergence of the nation-state in Western Europe produced the idea of a "national interest" superior to the interests of the individual subject and to which he was subservient. The purpose of public policy was to define what served the interests of the state and to confine and direct the actions of individuals into those channels and forms that served this national interest.

In spite of the demise of the divine right of kings and the rise of rights of man, and in spite of the refutation of mercantilism by the free-trade economists of the late 18th and 19th centuries, democratic governments continued to retain the notion of a national interest. But instead of being defined as serving the interests of the king, it was now postulated as serving "the people" of the nation as a whole. In the 20th century, public policy came to be assigned the tasks of guaranteeing full employment, generating economic growth, and directing investment and resources into those activities considered to foster the economic development considered most advantageous to "the nation."

Capitalism, therefore, has come to be viewed as compatible with and indeed even requiring activist government: a government that manipulates investment patterns through fiscal policy, regulates production, supervises competition through licensing and antitrust laws, stimulates exports by use of subsidies, and controls the purchase of imports with tariffs and quotas. The interventionist state, in the evolution of historical capitalism, has come to be considered the prerequisite for the maintenance of the market economy.

2. *Monetary Central Planning and the Rationale of Central Banking.* Whether in Europe or the United States, the application and practice of the principles of the market economy were subverted from the start with the existence of monetary central planning in the form of central banking. First seen as a device for assuring a steady flow of cheap money to finance the operations of government in excess of what those governments could extract from their subjects directly through taxation, monopolistic central banks were soon rationalized as the essential monetary institutions for economic stability. But as the German economist Gustav Stolper clearly explained in 1942 in his book, *This Age of Fable,*

"Hardly ever do the advocates of free capitalism realize how utterly their ideal was frustrated at the moment the state assumed control of the monetary system... A 'fire' capitalism with governmental responsibility for money and credit has lost its innocence. From that point on it is no longer a matter of principle but one of expediency how far one wishes or permits government interference to go. Money control is the supreme and most comprehensive of all governmental controls short of expropriation."

Once government controls the supply of money, it has the capacity to redistribute wealth; create inflations and cause industrial depressions; distort the structure of relative prices; generate misallocations of labor and capital throughout the economy; rationalize new governmental interventions in the face of the market "instability" that has actually been caused by the state's mismanagement of the money supply; manipulate the patterns of and the profits from international trade; and confiscate the income and wealth of millions through the hidden tax of rising prices arising from inflation.

3. The "Cruelty" of Capitalism and the Rationale for the Welfare State.
The privileged classes of pre-capitalist society hated the market. The individual was freed from subservience and obedience to the nobility, the aristocracy, and the landed interests. And for these privileged groups, the market meant loss of cheap labor, the disappearance of "proper respect" from their inferiors, and the economic uncertainty of changing market-generated circumstances. And for the socialists of the 19th century, capitalism was seen as the source of exploitation and economic insecurity for "the working class," who were dependent for their livelihood upon the apparent whims of the "capitalist class."

The welfare state became the solution to capitalism's supposed cruelty, a solution that created a vast and bloated welfare bureaucracy, made millions perpetual wards of a paternalistic state and drained society of the idea that freedom meant self-responsibility and mutual help through voluntary association.

The ideal and the principle of the market economy was never fulfilled. What is called capitalism today is a distorted, twisted and deformed system of increasingly limited market relationships as well as market processes hampered and repressed by state controls and regulations. And overlaying this entire system are the ideologies of 18th-century mercantilism, 19th-century socialism, and 20th-century welfare statism.

In this perverse development and evolution of "historical capitalism," the institutions necessary for a truly free-market economy have been either undermined or prevented from emerging. And the principles and actual meaning of a free-market economy have become increasingly misunderstood and lost. But it is the principles and the meaning of a free-market economy that must be rediscovered if liberty is to be saved and the burden of historical capitalism is to be overcome.

15
Why Socialism Must Fail
by Hans-Hermann Hoppe

Socialism and capitalism* offer radically different solutions to the problem posed by scarcity: everybody can't have everything they want when they want it, so how can we effectively decide who will own and control the resources we have? The chosen solution has profound implications. It can mean the difference between prosperity and impoverishment, voluntary exchange and political coercion, even totalitarianism and liberty.

The capitalist system solves the problem of scarcity by recognizing the right of private property. The first one to use a good is its owner. Others can acquire it only through trade and voluntary contracts. But until the owner of the property decides to make a contract to trade his property, he can do whatever he wants with it, so long as he does not interfere with or physically damage the property owned by others.

The socialist system attempts to solve the problem of ownership in a completely different way. Just as in capitalism, people can own consumer products. But in socialism, property which serves as the means of production are collectively owned. No person can own the machines and other

* Meaning the free market, not historical, State-regulated capitalism.

resources which go into producing consumption goods. Mankind, so to speak, owns them. If people use the means of production, they can do so only as caretakers for the entire community.

Economic law guarantees that harmful economic and sociological effects will always follow the socialization of the means of production. The socialist experiment will always end in failure.

First, socialism results in less investment, less saving, and lower standards of living. When socialism is initially imposed, property must be redistributed. The means of production are taken away from current users and producers and given to the community of caretakers. Even though the owners and users of the means of production acquired them through mutual consent from previous users, they are transferred to people who, at best, become users and producers of things they didn't own previously.

Under this system, previous owners are penalized in favor of new owners. The non-users, non-producers, and non-contractors of the means of production are favored by being promoted to the rank of caretaker over property which they had not previously used, produced, or contracted to use. Thus the income for the non-user, non-producer, and non-contractor rises. It is the same for the non-saver who benefits at the expense of the saver from whom the saved property is confiscated.

Clearly, then, if socialism favors the non-user, non-producer, non-contractor, and non-saver, it raises the costs that have to be born by users, producers, contractors, and savers. It is easy to see why there will be fewer people in these latter roles. There will be less original appropriation of natural resources, less production of new factors of production, and less contracting. There will be less preparation for the future because everyone's investment outlets dry up. There will be less saving and more consuming, less work and more leisure.

This adds up to fewer consumption goods being available for exchange, which reduces everyone's standard of living. If people are willing to take the risk, they will have to go underground to compensate for these losses.

Second, socialism results in inefficiencies, shortages, and prodigious waste. This is the insight of Ludwig von Mises who discovered that rational economic calculation is impossible under socialism. He showed that capital goods under socialism are at best used in the production of second-rate needs, and at worst, in production that satisfies no needs whatsoever.

Mises's insight is simple but extremely important: because the means of production under socialism cannot be sold, there are no market prices for them. The socialist caretaker cannot establish the monetary costs involved in using the resources or in making changes in the length of production processes. Nor can he compare these costs with the monetary income from sales. He is not allowed to take offers from others who want to use his means of production, so he cannot know what his foregone opportunities are. Without knowing foregone opportunities, he cannot know his costs. He cannot even know if the way he produces is efficient or inefficient, desired or undesired, rational or irrational. He cannot know whether he is satisfying less or more urgent needs of consumers.

In capitalism, money prices and free markets provide this information to the producer. But in socialism, there are no prices for capital goods and no opportunities for exchange. The caretaker is left in the dark. And because he can't know the status of his current production strategy, he can't know how to improve it. The less producers are able to calculate and engage in improvement, the more likely wastes and shortages become. In an economy where the consumer market for his products is very large, the producer's dilemma is even worse. It hardly needs to be pointed out: when there is no rational economic calculation, society will sink into progressively worsening impoverishment.

Third, socialism results in overutilization of the factors of production until they fall into disrepair and become vandalized. A private owner in capitalism has the right to sell his factor of production at any time and keep the revenues derived from the sale. So it is to his advantage to avoid lowering its capital value. Because he owns it, his objective is to maximize the value of the factor responsible for producing the goods and services he sells.

The status of the socialist caretaker is entirely different. He cannot sell his factor of production, so he has little or no incentive to insure that it retains its value. His incentive will instead be to increase the output of his factor of production without regard to its dwindling value. There is also the chance that if the caretaker perceives opportunities of employing the means of production for private purposes – like making goods for the black market – he will be encouraged to increase the output at the expense of capital values. No matter which way you look at it, under socialism without private ownership and free markets, producers will be inclined to consume capital values by overusing them. Capital consumption leads to impoverishment.

Fourth, socialism leads to a reduction in the quality of goods and services available for the consumer. Under capitalism, an individual businessman can maintain and expand his firm only if he recovers his costs of production. And since the demand for the firm's products depends on consumer evaluations of price and quality (price being one criterion of quality), product quality must be a constant concern of producers. This is only possible with private ownership and market exchange.

Things are entirely different under socialism. Not only are the means of production collectively owned, but so too is the income derived from the sale of the output. This is another way of saying that the producer's income has little or no connection with consumer evaluation of the producer's work. This fact, of course, is known by every producer.

The producer has no reason to make a special effort to improve the quality of his product. He will instead devote relatively less time and effort to producing what consumers want and spend more time doing what he wants. Socialism is a system that incites the producer to be lazy.

Fifth, socialism leads to the politicization of society. Hardly anything can be worse for the production of wealth.

Socialism, at least its Marxist version, says its goal is complete equality. The Marxists observe that once you allow private property in the means of production, you allow differences. If I own resource A, then you do not own it and our relationship toward resource A becomes different and unequal. By abolishing private property in the means of production with one stroke, say the Marxists, everyone becomes co-owner of everything. This reflects everyone's equal standing as a human being.

The reality is much different. Declaring everyone a co-owner of everything only nominally solves differences in ownership. It does not solve the real underlying problem: there remain differences in the power to control what is done with resources.

In capitalism, the person who owns a resource can also control what is done with it. In a socialized economy, this isn't true because there is no longer any owner. Nonetheless the problem of control remains. Who is going to decide what is to be done with what? Under socialism, there is only one way: people settle their disagreements over the control of property by superimposing one will upon another. As long as there are differences, people will settle them through political means.

If people want to improve their income under socialism they have to move toward a more highly valued position in the hierarchy of caretakers. That takes political talent. Under such a system, people will have to spend less time and effort developing their productive skills and more time and effort improving their political talents.

As people shift out of their roles as producers and users of resources, we find that their personalities change. They no longer cultivate the ability to anticipate situations of scarcity, to take up productive opportunities, to be aware of technological possibilities, to anticipate changes in consumer demand, and to develop strategies of marketing. They no longer have to be able to initiate, to work, and to respond to the needs of others.

Instead, people develop the ability to assemble public support for their own position and opinion through means of persuasion, demagoguery, and intrigue, through promises, bribes, and threats. Different people rise to the top under socialism than under capitalism. The higher on the socialist hierarchy you look, the more you will find people who are too incompetent to do the job they are supposed to do. It is no hindrance in a caretaker-politician's career to be dumb, indolent, inefficient, and uncaring. He only needs superior political skills. This too contributes to the impoverishment of society.

The United States is not fully socialized, but already we see the disastrous effects of a politicized society as our own politicians continue to encroach on the rights of private property owners. All the impoverishing effects of socialism are with us in the U.S.: reduced levels of investment and saving, the misallocation of resources, the overutilization and vandalization of factors of production, and the inferior quality of products and services. And these are only tastes of life under total socialism.

16
Agorist Living
by Nicholas Hooton

The idea of joining the Libertarian Party tempted me years ago when I first discovered libertarian philosophy, as I'm sure it has tempted many before and since. The Party website stared me in the face, and with a few clicks and keystrokes I could be a card-carrying member of an organized body of liberty-minded people.

Eventually, the same rational thought processes and self-examination that led me to libertarianism revealed to me the true motives behind my desire to join: a base psychological need for attention and belonging. I'm proud to report that I left the website unaffiliated, as I had always been before and have been ever since.

I later learned just how close I came to never knowing the peace and prosperity that comes with an understanding and practice of anarchism*. The temptation had not been one of simply belonging, but of obtaining power – political power, in this case. I knew that, if I ever ran for public office, I would most likely need the financial backing of a political party, and running under a Democrat or Republican ticket would have been downright hypocritical.

---

* Anarchism is properly and here defined as: the absence of the State.

This thinking occurred, of course, when the last vestiges of statism still clouded my vision as the remaining threads and rags of a blindfold that had been clawed at for years. I still considered the Constitution to be sacred, limited government to be the goal, and the social contract to be the only way life and property could be protected.

"There are two methods, or means, and only two, whereby man's needs and desires can be satisfied," I later learned from noted social critic Albert Jay Nock. "One is the production and exchange of wealth; this is the economic means. The other is the uncompensated appropriation of wealth produced by others; this is the political means... The positive testimony of history is that the State invariably had its origin in conquest and confiscation. No primitive State known to history originated in any other manner."

For many years, "anarcho-capitalists" (under the direction of Mr. Libertarian himself, Murray Rothbard) have attempted to work within the political means to bring down the State. From the inception of the Libertarian Party up until its remaining anarchists were disinvited by means of the "Denver Accord", to the attention-getting attempts at the Presidency by libertarian poster child Ron Paul, anarcho-capitalists have put their trust in the very political machine they reject. These attempts have been fruitless, of course. The American political machine is stronger than it has ever been, arguably more powerful than any State in man's history; and the Libertarian Party has become such an impotent hiss and by-word that it no longer garners even comedic targeting.

While "Partyarchs" were busy sacrificing principle on the alter of political intrigue, the "new libertarian left" was born. Some called themselves voluntaryists and rejected every political means to obtaining libertarian ends. Voluntaryists are noted for abstention from voting, some even claiming it to be immoral. They are also known for peaceful non-cooperation. Nowhere has this strategy been better explored and implemented, however, than in the school of thought within this movement that calls itself "agorism".

Rothbard's libertarian manifesto published in 1973 offered little in the realm of strategy; indeed, the subject took up only a few pages in an epilogue and centered mostly on educating key groups in society about the philosophy of liberty. Seven years after (and most likely in response to) Rothbard's work, Samuel E. Konkin III published his *New Libertarian Manifesto* in which he laid out the groundwork of agorism, his philosophical extension and fulfillment of libertarian moral philosophy.

In this work, Konkin described what he called "counter-economics" or "all (non-coercive) human action committed in defiance of the State." Agorism is "the consistent integration of libertarian theory with counter-economic practice." Counter-economics includes black market activities – illegal activities that are not violent or invasive and therefore "victimless" – and grey market activities – activities that are not illegal but conducted in a manner prohibited by the State.

Many are shocked when they first learn of counter-economics. Engaging in illegal activities isn't how they envisioned their political activism or the way they live their lives; but the fact is that nearly everyone has engaged or regularly engages in such activities. If you've ever had a lemonade stand or a yard sale or sold something online without complying with all applicable regulatory and tax code mandates, you're a counter-economist. If you've ever used an expired prescription or someone else's prescription or smoked weed, you're a counter-economist. If you've ever been so much as a penny off on your income tax return, even without knowing it, you're a counter-economist.

My earliest lessons in counter-economics were taught to me by my dad, although I didn't know it until years later. He taught me about buying and selling automobiles to and from trusted acquaintances. In such transactions, the seller could provide the buyer with a bill of sale stating a greatly reduced sale price in order to reduce or eliminate the buyer's sales tax burden.

As a salesman, my dad went on more road trips than I can remember and frequently brought me along for company. I remember that he had a radar detector to avoid speeding tickets. He also had a CB radio with which he would converse with trucking convoys to avoid speed traps and the like. He taught me the lingo and helped me to understand how to earn the trust of the other CB operators by developing a reputable handle.

Such activities as these and many others offer a consistent and realistic strategy for undermining and ultimately replacing the State. As agorists engage in under-the-radar commerce with other agorists and liberty-minded merchants, organizations such as barter networks, cooperatives, mutual aid associations, local exchange trading systems, arbitration firms, and security networks can slowly and surely provide viable alternatives to services ostensibly provided by the State. Prosperity will follow.

One of the sublimely emancipating realizations one has in living the agorist life is one that seems to have escaped Konkin and other early agorist thinkers, and that is that a free society is not some far-off goal toward which we are working. It is not an unattainable utopia, or even an attainable arrangement many centuries down the road. No, "free society" is a tautology. Every society is free, as is every market. I will explain, because this notion, I believe, is key to consistency in libertarian philosophy, as well as for each individual to obtain the full measure of peace and prosperity that agorist living can provide.

A society is simply a group of two or more individuals, and a market is simply a place or system wherein two or more individuals engage in mutual exchange. If libertarian moral philosophy is valid, if the principle of non-aggression is indeed a universal ethical principle by which human interaction ought to be guided, then it is true at all times and in all places, in all societies and markets.

For example, the geographical area known as North America contains many free societies and free markets in which several well organized criminal syndicates known as States operate unchallenged. They are currently too powerful to be repelled by any private security firm or syndicate, and they have used mass propaganda to obtain the sanction of most of their victims.

I don't think any libertarian is so naïve as to assume that no crime exists in free markets. Libertarians advocate freedom to pursue voluntary solutions to crime. If a free market is a market in which zero crime or aggression occurs, then there will never be a free market, and we strive for it in vain. If we respond to criticisms of free markets by claiming that "we don't live in a free market", then we are admitting that the non-aggression principle actually does not apply in our society, and therefore the State's actions are perfectly legitimate.

To know that you are free, that you always have been, and that you always will be, is one of the most peaceful and liberating ideas I have ever uncovered. You are free. Any aggression committed against you by the State or by any other person or organization is illegitimate, and you have the right to defend yourself. The question isn't what you will do to achieve a free society. The question is what you will do, each and every day, to respond to the significant criminal threat extant in this free society of yours *right now*. I submit that agorism is the only philosophically consistent answer to that question.

Free Market Resources

Books

Economics in One Lesson, by Henry Hazlitt

"A million copy seller, [this book] is a classic economic primer. But it is also much more, having become a fundamental influence on modern [free market] economics of the type espoused by Ron Paul and others. Concise and instructive, it is also deceptively prescient and far-reaching in its efforts to dissemble economic fallacies that are so prevalent they have almost become a new orthodoxy." (RandomHouse.com)

The Free Market Reader, edited by Llewelyn H. Rockwell, Jr.

"What you will find here are one hundred plus short essays on every topic related to free-market economics, all from the years of the monthly publication of *The Free Market*, when Murray Rothbard was writing a regular column. His work all appears here, but so do the writings of many other top thinkers such as Mises, Block, Rockwell, Ron Paul, William Peterson, Lawrence Reed, Richard Ebeling, Hans Hoppe, and many more. Topics include privatization, socialism around the world, economic history, debt and deficits, fiat money and exchange rates, trade and protectionism, Keynesianism, supply-side economics, and many other topics. It makes for great reading, one essay at a time. It is the sort of book you can dip into and out of very quickly, and gain a great deal of insight as you do." (Mises.org)

Defending the Undefendable, by Walter Block

This book "is among the most famous of the great defenses of victimless crimes and controversial economic practices, from profiteering and gouging to bribery and blackmail. However, beneath the surface, this book is also an outstanding work of microeconomic theory that explains the workings of economic forces in everyday events and affairs." (Mises.org)

Basic Economics, by Thomas Sowell

This book "is a citizen's guide to economics – for those who want to understand how the economy works but have no interest in jargon or equations. Sowell reveals the general principles behind any kind of economy – capitalist, socialist, feudal, and so on. In readable language, he shows how to critique economic policies in terms of the incentives they create, rather than the goals they proclaim."

Free Market Economics: A Reader, by Bettina Bien Greaves

"Bettina Bien Greaves put this volume together as a one-stop primer in economics that includes the best economic writing she had run across. In some ways, the choices are brilliant. They are arranged by topic to cover the division of labor, prices, profits, property, competition, saving and investment, environment, antitrust, money and banking, advertising and marketing, and more. Authors include Read, Mises, Bastiat, Greaves, Kirzner, Watts, Hazlitt, and many other writers." (Mises.org)

A Theory of Socialism and Capitalism, by Hans Hoppe

"Here is Hans Hoppe's first treatise in English - actually his first book in English - and the one that put him on the map as a social thinker and economist to watch. He argued that there are only two possible archetypes in economic affairs: socialism and capitalism. All systems are combinations of those two types. The capitalist model he defines is the pure protection of private property, free association, and exchange – no exceptions. All deviations from that ideal are species of socialism, with public ownership and interference with trade." (Mises.org)

Man, Economy, & State, by Murray Rothbard

This book "provides a sweeping presentation of Austrian economic theory, a reconstruction of many aspects of that theory, a rigorous criticism of alternative schools, and an inspiring look at a science of liberty that concerns nearly everything and should concern everyone." (Mises.org)

Human Action, by Ludwig von Mises

This "is the best defense of capitalism ever written. It covers basic economics through the most advanced material. Reading this book is the best way you could ever dream up to learn economics. Every attempt to study economics should include a thorough examination of this book." (Mises.org)

An Agorist Primer, by Samuel E. Konkin, III

This book is a "a primer on all the important aspects of Agorism and Counter-Economics: how they work together to enable you to free yourself and expand freedom to your friends, family, and the world!"

Websites

Mises.org, "The Ludwig von Mises Institute was founded in 1982 as the research and educational center of classical liberalism, libertarian political theory, and the Austrian School of economics. It serves as the world's leading provider of educational materials, conferences, media, and literature in support of the tradition of thought represented by Ludwig von Mises and the school of thought he enlivened and carried forward during the 20th century, which has now blossomed into a massive international movement of students, professors, professionals, and people in all walks of life. It seeks a radical shift in the intellectual climate as the foundation for a renewal of the free and prosperous commonwealth."

FEE.org, The Foundation for Economic Education, one of the oldest free-market organizations in the United States, was founded in 1946 by Leonard E. Read to study and advance the freedom philosophy. FEE's mission is to offer the most consistent case for the "first principles" of freedom: the sanctity of private property, individual liberty, the rule of law, the free market, and the moral superiority of individual choice and responsibility over coercion."

TheFreemanOnline.org, *"The Freeman: Ideas on Liberty*, is the flagship publication of the Foundation for Economic Education and one of the oldest and most respected journals of liberty in America. For more than 50 years it has uncompromisingly defended the ideals of the free society.

EconomicPolicyJournal.com provides daily commentary on all things economics from an Austrian School, free market perspective.

Agorism.info is the biggest web portal for all things counter-economics. You'll find all the best material and books on Agorism, for free. "In a market anarchist society, law and security would be provided by market actors instead of political institutions. Agorists recognize that that situation can not develop through political reform. Instead, it will arise as a result of market processes."

Section Four – Education

17
The Trouble with Traditional Schooling
by Vahram G. Diehl

Traditional concepts and applications of learning have generally been one-sided. The "teacher" transmits information in the form of conclusions through words and images, while the "students" are expected to act as flawless receivers and adopters of these conclusions; they are to memorize them until the appropriate moment of testing commences and then to regurgitate the same words and images in a context that demonstrates the transmission was mostly successful. The more complete the regurgitation, the higher grade a student will receive and accordingly be considered smarter and more capable.

With this style of information soaking and squeezing, the ratio of students to teachers can be rather high and still function with moderate success. When the only role of the teacher is to serve as a one-way streaming thoroughfare for information and the students are relegated to docile receptacles of this information, dozens or even hundreds of passive students can be accommodated by one active teacher. This creates an active/passive class separation between the two groups; the teacher's only job is to actively teach, the students' only job is to passively learn. In this system of imposed homogeneity, the naturally faster learners are made to sacrifice their own progress so that others might catch up; the naturally slower learners are made to cut corners to create the appearance of equality.

This state of extended passive receptivity gives rise to problems in many students whose minds do not take well to the building of new logical constructs in such a dormant mental state. Even in the seemingly passive act of reading of a book, it is the mind of the reader that actively instigates the advancement of each new word or the turning of the page, and it is the will of the reader to retain the information presented. The inability to learn without active engagement is readily obvious in young children who will typically only participate and pay attention when they are allowed to somehow actively engage in the learning process, which they eagerly do.

For some strange reason, it has become expected that after a few years of gentle conditioning to passivity and weaning away from genuine educational interaction that students of a certain age will easily do away with their juvenile traits of curiosity and enthusiasm. The only function this serves is that they may become more easily manageable for the sole teacher supplied to keep them in line and to efficiently expedite the information transmission process. The students who have the most difficult time relinquishing their natural temperaments toward action are labeled as feebleminded and troublemakers, though human history has shown that the most brilliant and ambitious of men are often the ones who retain their natural luster and are subject to these labels and ostracisms.

When schooling is passive and not incited by the curiosity of the students, it usually results in very fragmented and incomplete education. Teachers and rulers determine for the students which arbitrarily divided subcategories of information are most pertinent and valuable to learn, in what sequence they will be learned, and on what schedule. When an education is compartmentalized and centrally planned like this, students are given content with no context. They come to see the world in segmented chunks of the loosely known details, intermittently obscured by gaping holes of the bluntly unknown. This happens in place of an active and voluntary education, where every new piece of information would fall into logical consistency with and compliment every previous piece of information in the gradual building of an increasingly accurate worldview, like a lens slowly coming into focus. Instead, old topics are seen as outdated and irrelevant compared to whatever the favored subcategory of the moment happens to be.

Ultimately, the passive learners become highly refined specialists on one particular sliver of reality, while largely ignoring the rest of existence and passing off all other knowledge as someone else's field and responsibility; nothing is integrated with past knowledge and the student excels only at regurgitating and applying professionally the same conclusions that were presented to him during his schooling.

This overall process when applied from early youth onward has a cumulatively dehumanizing effect on the students. The long hours required to be at school necessarily bestow upon teachers and other administrative staff a partial parental role over the young, without qualification or consent. They understandably fail to perform the full spectrum of tasks required for the upbringing of a healthy and capable adult human, including but not limited to providing proper nutrition, emotional support and expression, natural socialization, ethics, passion, compassion, love, reason, nonviolent communication, etc. The students are made to sacrifice a major part of the natural maturing process so that they will learn the subjects deemed appropriate by society and their teachers. This is in no way a fair trade.

The uniformity in schooling destroys individuality and creativity in humans. As all children are taught to think in the same socially acceptable ways, comparatively few will go on to have vastly original insights and create unique works of art. Because the teaching styles are not tailored to natural individual styles of learning and coming to understand the world, most will be made to forfeit their own innate ways of thinking and to adopt the same intellectual and emotional methods of everyone else. Progress for all of civilization itself is stifled because most people are only capable of replicating what they are already familiar with and few will seek new and radical changes in the way things are done, however much better those changes might be.

Evolution is driven by the enormous diversity of traits in effect and actively being replicated. By restricting diversity, one cannot avoid restricting evolution itself.

18
Schooling: The Hidden Agenda
by Daniel Quinn

A Talk Given at the Houston Unschoolers Group Family Learning Conference.

I suspect that not everyone in this audience knows who I am or why I've been invited to speak to you today. After all, I've never written a book or even an article about homeschooling or unschooling. I've been called a number of things: a futurist, a planetary philosopher, an anthropologist from Mars. Recently I was introduced to an audience as a cultural critic, and I think this probably says it best. As you'll see, in my talk to you today, I will be trying to place schooling and unschooling in the larger context of our cultural history and that of our species as well.

For those of you who are unfamiliar with my work, I should begin by explaining what I mean by "our culture". Rather than burden you with a definition, I'll give you a simple test that you can use wherever you go in the world. If the food in that part of the world is under lock and key, and the people who live there have to work to get it, then you're among people of our culture. If you happen to be in a jungle in the interior of Brazil or

New Guinea, however, you'll find that the food is not under lock and key. It's simply out there for the taking, and anyone who wants some can just go and get it. The people who live in these areas, often called aboriginals, stone-age peoples, or tribal peoples clearly belong to a culture radically different from our own.

I first began to focus my attention on the peculiarities of our own culture in the early 1960s, when I went to work for what was then a cutting-edge publisher of educational materials, Science Research Associates. I was in my mid-twenties and as thoroughly acculturated as any senator, bus driver, movie star, or medical doctor. My fundamental acceptances about the universe and humanity's place in it were rock-solid and thoroughly conventional.

But it was a stressful time to be alive, in some ways even more stressful than the present. Many people nowadays realize that human life may well be in jeopardy, but this jeopardy exists in some vaguely defined future, twenty or fifty or a hundred years hence. But in those coldest days of the Cold War everyone lived with the realization that a nuclear holocaust could occur literally at any second, without warning. It was very realistically the touch of a button away.

Human life would not be entirely snuffed out in a holocaust of this kind. In a way, it would be even worse than that. In a matter of hours, we would be thrown back not just to the Stone Age but to a level of almost total helplessness. In the Stone Age, after all, people lived perfectly well without supermarkets, shopping malls, hardware stores, and all the elaborate systems that keep these places stocked with the things we need. Within hours our cities would disintegrate into chaos and anarchy, and the necessities of life would vanish from store shelves, never to be replaced. Within days famine would be widespread.

Skills that are taken for granted among Stone Age peoples would be unknown to the survivors – the ability to differentiate between edible and inedible foods growing in their own environment, the ability to stalk, kill, dress, and preserve game animals, and most important the ability to make tools from available materials. How many of you know how to cure a hide? How to make a rope from scratch? How to flake a stone tool? Much less how to smelt metal from raw ore. Commonplace skills of the Paleolithic, developed over thousands of years, would be lost arts.

All this was freely acknowledged by people who didn't doubt for a moment that we were living the way humans were meant to live from the beginning of time, who didn't doubt for a moment that the things our children were learning in school were exactly the things they should be learning.

I'd been hired at SRA to work on a major new mathematics program that had been under development for several years in Cleveland. In my first year, we were going to publish the kindergarten and first-grade programs. In the second year, we'd publish the second-grade program, in the third year, the third-grade program, and so on. Working on the kindergarten and first-grade programs, I observed something that I thought was truly remarkable. In these grades, children spend most of their time learning things that no one growing up in our culture could possibly avoid learning. For example, they learn the names of the primary colors. Wow, just imagine missing school on the day when they were learning blue. You'd spend the rest of your life wondering what color the sky is. They learn to tell time, to count, and to add and subtract, as if anyone could possibly fail to learn these things in this culture. And of course they make the beginnings of learning how to read. I'll go out on a limb here and suggest an experiment. Two classes of 30 kids, taught identically and given the identical text materials throughout their school experience, but one class is given no instruction in reading at all and the other is given the usual instruction. Call it the Quinn Conjecture: both classes will test the same on reading skills at the end of twelve years. I feel safe in making this conjecture because ultimately kids learn to read the same way they learn to speak, by hanging around people who read and by wanting to be able to do what these people do.

It occurred to me at this time to ask this question: Instead of spending two or three years teaching children things they will inevitably learn anyway, why not teach them some things they will not inevitably learn and that they would actually enjoy learning at this age? How to navigate by the stars, for example. How to tan a hide. How to distinguish edible foods from inedible foods. How to build a shelter from scratch. How to make tools from scratch. How to make a canoe. How to track animals – all the forgotten but still valuable skills that our civilization is actually built on.

Of course I didn't have to vocalize this idea to anyone to know how it would be received. Being thoroughly acculturated, I could myself explain why it was totally inane. The way we live is the way humans were meant to live from the beginning of time, and our children were being prepared to enter that life. Those who came before us were savages, little more than brutes. Those who continue to live the way our ancestors lived are savages, little more than brutes. The world is well rid of them, and we're well rid of every vestige of them, including their ludicrously primitive skills.

Our children were being prepared in school to step boldly into the only fully human life that had ever existed on this planet. The skills they were acquiring in school would bring them not only success but deep personal fulfillment on every level. What did it matter if they never did more than work in some mind-numbing factory job? They could parse a sentence! They could explain to you the difference between a Petrarchan sonnet and a Shakespearean sonnet! They could extract a square root! They could show you why the square of the two sides of a right triangle were equal to the square of the hypotenuse! They could analyze a poem! They could explain to you how a bill passes congress! They could very possibly trace for you the economic causes of the Civil War. They had read Melville and Shakespeare, so why would they not now read Dostoevsky and Racine, Joyce and Beckett, Faulkner and O'Neill? But above all else, of course, the citizen's education – grades K to twelve – prepared children to be fully-functioning participants in this great civilization of ours. The day after their graduation exercises, they were ready to stride confidently toward any goal they might set themselves.

Of course, then, as now, everyone knew that the citizen's education was doing no such thing. It was perceived then – as now – that there was something strangely wrong with the schools. They were failing – and failing miserably – at delivering on these enticing promises. Ah well, teachers weren't being paid enough, so what could you expect? We raised teachers' salaries – again and again and again – and still the schools failed. Well, what could you expect? The schools were physically decrepit, lightless, and uninspiring. We built new ones – tens of thousands, hundreds of thousands of them – and still the schools failed. Well, what could you expect? The curriculum was antiquated and irrelevant. We modernized the curriculum, did our damnedest to make it relevant – and still the schools failed. Every week – then as now – you could read about some bright new idea that would surely "fix" whatever was wrong with our schools: the open classroom, team teaching, back to basics, more homework, less homework, no homework – I couldn't begin to enumerate them all. Hundreds of these bright ideas were implemented – thousands of them were implemented – and still the schools failed.

Within our cultural matrix, every medium tells us that the schools exist to prepare children for a successful and fulfilling life in our civilization (and are therefore failing). This is beyond argument, beyond doubt, beyond question. In *Ishmael* I said that the voice of Mother Culture speaks to us from every newspaper and magazine article, every movie, every sermon, every book, every parent, every teacher, every school administrator, and what she has to say about the schools is that they exist to prepare children for a successful and fulfilling life in our civilization (and are therefore failing). Once we step outside our cultural matrix, this voice no longer fills our ears and we're free to ask some new questions. Suppose the schools aren't failing? Suppose they're doing exactly what we really want them to do – but don't wish to examine and acknowledge?

Granted that the schools do a poor job of preparing children for a successful and fulfilling life in our civilization, but what things do they do excellently well? Well, to begin with, they do a superb job of keeping young people out of the job market. Instead of becoming wage-earners at age twelve or fourteen, they remain consumers only – and they consume billions of dollars worth of merchandise, using money that their parents earn. Just imagine what would happen to our economy if overnight the high schools closed their doors. Instead of having fifty million active consumers out there, we would suddenly have fifty million unemployed youth. It would be nothing short of an economic catastrophe.

Of course the situation was very different two hundred years ago, when we were still a primarily agrarian society. Youngsters were expected and needed to become workers at age ten, eleven, and twelve. For the masses, a fourth, fifth, or sixth-grade education was deemed perfectly adequate. But as the character of our society changed, fewer youngsters were needed for farm work, and the enactment of child-labor laws soon made it impossible to put ten-, eleven-, and twelve-year-olds to work in factories. It was necessary to keep them off the streets – and where better than in schools? Naturally, new material had to be inserted into the curriculum to fill up the time. It didn't much matter what it was. Have them memorize the capitals of every state. Have them memorize the principle products of every state. Have them learn the steps a bill takes in passing Congress. No one wondered or cared if these were things kids wanted to know or needed to know – or would ever need to know. No one wondered or ever troubled to find out if the material being added to the curriculum was retained. The educators didn't want to know, and, really, what difference would it make? It didn't matter that, once learned, they were immediately forgotten. It filled up some time. The law decreed that an eighth-grade education was essential for every citizen, and so curriculum writers provided material needed for an eighth-grade education.

During the Great Depression it became urgently important to keep young people off the job market for as long as possible, and so it came to be understood that a twelfth-grade education was essential for every citizen. As before, it didn't much matter what was added to fill up the time, so long as it was marginally plausible. Let's have them learn how to analyze a poem, even if they never read another one in their whole adult life. Let's have them read a great classic novel, even if they never read another one in their whole adult life. Let's have them study world history, even if it all just goes in one ear and out the other. Let's have them study Euclidean geometry, even if two years later they couldn't prove a single theorem to save their lives. All these things and many, many more were of course justified on the basis that they would contribute to the success and rich fulfillment that these children would experience as adults. Except, of course, that it didn't. But no one wanted to know about that. No one would have dreamed of testing young people five years after graduation to find out how much of it they'd retained. No one would have dreamed of asking them how useful it had been to them in realistic terms or how much it had contributed to their success and fulfillment as humans. What would be the point of asking them to evaluate their education? What did they know about it, after all? They were just high school graduates, not professional educators.

At the end of the Second World War, no one knew what the economic future was going to be like. With the disappearance of the war industries, would the country fall back into the pre-war depression slump? The word began to go out that the citizen's education should really include four years of college. Everyone should go to college. As the economy continued to grow, however, this injunction began to be softened. Four years of college would sure be good for you, but it wasn't part of the citizen's education, which ultimately remained a twelfth-grade education.

It was in the good years following the war, when there were often more jobs than workers to fill them, that our schools began to be perceived as failing. With ready workers in demand, it was apparent that kids were coming out of school without knowing much more than the sixth-grade graduates of a century ago. They'd "gone through" all the material that had been added to fill up the time – analyzed poetry, diagramed sentences, proved theorems, solved for x, plowed through thousands of pages of history and literature, written bushels of themes, but for the most part they retained almost none of it – and of how much use would it be to them if they had?

From a business point of view, these high-school graduates were barely employable.

But of course by then the curriculum had achieved the status of scripture, and it was too late to acknowledge that the program had never been designed to be useful. The educators' response to the business community was, "We just have to give the kids more of the same – more poems to analyze, more sentences to diagram, more theorems to prove, more equations to solve, more pages of history and literature to read, more themes to write, and so on." No one was about to acknowledge that the program had been set up to keep young people off the job market – and that it had done a damn fine job of that at least.

But keeping young people off the job market is only half of what the schools do superbly well. By the age of thirteen or fourteen, children in aboriginal societies – tribal societies – have completed what we, from our point of view, would call their "education". They're ready to "graduate" and become adults. In these societies, what this means is that their survival value is 100%. All their elders could disappear overnight, and there would not be chaos, anarchy, and famine among these new adults. They would be able to carry on without a hitch. None of the skills and technologies practiced by their parents would be lost. If they wanted to, they could live quite independently of the tribal structure in which they were reared.

But the last thing we want our children to be able to do is to live independently of our society. We don't want our graduates to have a survival value of 100%, because this would make them free to opt out of our carefully constructed economic system and do whatever they please. We don't want them to do whatever they please, we want them to have exactly two choices (assuming they're not independently wealthy). Get a job or go to college. Either choice is good for us, because we need a constant supply of entry-level workers and we also need doctors, lawyers, physicists, mathematicians, psychologists, geologists, biologists, school teachers, and so on. The citizen's education accomplishes this almost without fail. Ninety-nine point nine percent of our high school graduates make one of these two choices.

And it should be noted that our high-school graduates are reliably entry-level workers. We want them to have to grab the lowest rung on the ladder. What sense would it make to give them skills that would make it possible for them to grab the second rung or the third rung? Those are the rungs their older brothers and sisters are reaching for. And if this year's graduates were reaching for the second or third rungs, who would be doing the work at the bottom? The business people who do the hiring constantly complain that graduates know absolutely nothing, have virtually no useful skills at all. But in truth how could it be otherwise?

So you see that our schools are not failing, they're just succeeding in ways we prefer not to see. Turning out graduates with no skills, with no survival value, and with no choice but to work or starve are not flaws of the system, they are features of the system. These are the things the system must do to keep things going on as they are.

The need for schooling is bolstered by two well-entrenched pieces of cultural mythology. The first and most pernicious of these is that children will not learn unless they're compelled to – in school. It is part of the mythology of childhood itself that children hate learning and will avoid it at all costs. Of course, anyone who has had a child knows what an absurd lie this is. From infancy onward, children are the most fantastic learners in the world. If they grow up in a family in which four languages are spoken, they will be speaking four languages by the time they're three or four years old – without a day of schooling, just by hanging around the members of their family, because they desperately want to be able to do the things they do. Anyone who has had a child knows that they are tirelessly curious. As soon as they're able to ask questions, they ask questions incessantly, often driving their parents to distraction. Their curiosity extends to everything they can reach, which is why every parent soon learns to put anything breakable, anything dangerous, anything untouchable up high – and if possible behind lock and key. We all know the truth of the joke about those childproof bottle caps: those are the kind that only children can open.

People who imagine that children are resistant to learning have a non-existent understanding of how human culture developed in the first place. Culture is no more and no less than the totality of learned behavior and information that is passed from one generation to the next. The desire to eat is not transmitted by culture, but knowledge about how edible foods are found, collected, and processed is transmitted by culture. Before the invention of writing, whatever was not passed on from one generation to the next was simply lost, no matter what it was – a technique, a song, a detail of history. Among aboriginal peoples – those we haven't destroyed – the transmission between generations is remarkably complete, but of course not 100% complete. There will always be trivial details of personal history that the older generation takes to its grave. But the vital material is never lost.

This comes about because the desire to learn is hardwired into the human child just the way that the desire to reproduce is hardwired into the human adult. It's genetic. If there was ever a strain of humans whose children were not driven to learn, they're long gone, because they could not be culture-bearers.

Children don't have to be motivated to learn everything they can about the world they inhabit, they're absolutely driven to learn it. By the onset of puberty, children in aboriginal societies have unfailingly learned everything they need to function as adults.

Think of it this way. In the most general terms, the human biological clock is set for two alarms. When the first alarm goes off, at birth, the clock chimes learn, learn, learn, learn, learn. When the second alarm goes off, at the onset of puberty, the clock chimes mate, mate, mate, mate, mate. The chime that goes learn, learn, learn never disappears entirely, but it becomes relatively faint at the onset of puberty. At that point, children cease to want to follow their parents around in the learning dance. Instead, they want to follow each other around in the mating dance.

We, of course, in our greater wisdom have decreed that the biological clock regulated by our genes must be ignored.

What sells most people on the idea of school is the fact that the un-schooled child learns what it wants to learn when it wants to learn it. This is intolerable to them, because they're convinced that children don't want to learn anything at all – and they point to school children to prove it. What they fail to recognize is that the learning curve of preschool children swoops upward like a mountain – but quickly levels off when they enter school. By the third or fourth grade it's completely flat for most kids. Learning, such as it is, has become a boring, painful experience they'd love to be able to avoid if they could. But there's another reason why people abhor the idea of children learning what they want to learn when they want to learn it. They won't all learn the same things! Some of them will never learn to analyze a poem! Some of them will never learn to parse a sentence or write a theme! Some of them will never read Julius Caesar! Some will never learn geometry! Some will never dissect a frog! Some will never learn how a bill passes Congress! Well, of course, this is too horrible to imagine. It doesn't matter that 90% of these students will never read another poem or another play by Shakespeare in their lives. It doesn't matter that 90% of them will never have occasion to parse another sentence or write another theme in their lives. It doesn't matter that 90% retain no functional knowledge of the geometry or algebra they studied. It doesn't matter that 90% never have any use for whatever knowledge they were supposed to gain from dissecting a frog. It doesn't matter that 90% graduate without having the vaguest idea how a bill passes Congress. All that matters is that they've gone through it!

The people who are horrified by the idea of children learning what they want to learn when they want to learn it have not accepted the very elementary psychological fact that people (all people, of every age) remember the things that are important to them – the things they need to know – and forget the rest. I am a living witness to this fact. I went to one of the best prep schools in the country and graduated fourth in my class, and I doubt very much if I could now get a passing grade in more than two or three of the dozens of courses I took. I studied classical Greek for two solid years, and now would be unable to read aloud a single sentence.

One final argument people advance to support the idea that children need all the schooling we give them is that there is vastly more material to be learned today than there was in prehistoric times or even a century ago. Well, there is of course vastly more material that can be learned, but we all know perfectly well that it isn't being taught in grades K to twelve. Whole vast new fields of knowledge exist today – things no one even heard of a century ago: astrophysics, biochemistry, paleobiology, aeronautics, particle physics, ethology, cytopathology, neurophysiology – I could list them for hours. But are these the things that we have jammed into the K-12 curriculum because everyone needs to know them? Certainly not. The idea is absurd. The idea that children need to be schooled for a long time because there is so much that can be learned is absurd. If the citizen's education were to be extended to include everything that can be learned, it wouldn't run to grade twelve, it would run to grade twelve thousand, and no one would be able to graduate in a single lifetime.

I know of course that there is no one in this audience who needs to be sold on the virtues of homeschooling or unschooling. I hope, however, that I may have been able to add some philosophical, historical, anthropological, and biological foundation for your conviction that school ain't all it's cracked up to be.

19
The Right to Control One's Learning
by John Holt

Young people should have the right to control and direct their own learning; that is, to decide what they want to learn, and when, where, how, how much, how fast, and with what help they want to learn it. To be still more specific, I want them to have the right to decide if, when, how much, and by whom they want to be *taught* and the right to decide whether they want to learn in a school and if so which one and for how much of the time. No human right, except the right to life itself, is more fundamental than this. A person's freedom of learning is part of his freedom of thought, even more basic than his freedom of speech. If we take from someone his right to decide what he will be curious about, we destroy his freedom of thought. We say, in effect, you must think not about what interests and concerns you, but about what interests and concerns us.

We might call this the right of curiosity, the right to ask whatever questions are most important to us. As adults, we assume that we have the right to decide what does or does not interest us, what we will look into and what we will leave alone. We take this right for granted, cannot imagine that it might be taken away from us. Indeed, as far as I know, it has never been written into any body of law. Even the writers of our Constitution did not mention it. They thought it was enough to guarantee citizens the freedom of speech and the freedom to spread their ideas as widely as they wished and could. It did not occur to them that even the most tyrannical government would try to control people's minds, what they thought and knew. That idea was to come later, under the benevolent guise of compulsory universal education.

This right of each of us to control our own learning is now in danger. When we put into our laws the highly authoritarian notion that someone should and could decide what all young people were to learn and, beyond that, could do whatever might seem necessary (which now includes dosing them with drugs) to compel them to learn it, we took a long step down a very steep and dangerous path. The requirement that a child go to school, for about six hours a day, 180 days a year, for about ten years, whether or not he learns anything there, whether or not he already knows it or could learn it faster or better somewhere else, is such a gross violation of civil liberties that few adults would stand for it. But the child who resists is treated as a criminal.

The right I ask for the young is a right that I want to preserve for the rest of us, the right to decide what goes into our minds. This is much more than the right to decide whether or when or how much to go to school or what school you want to go to. That right is important, but it is only part of a much larger and more fundamental right, which I might call the right to learn, as opposed to being *educated*, i.e. made to learn what someone else thinks would be good for you. It is not just compulsory schooling but compulsory *education* that I oppose and want to do away with.

That children might have the control of their own learning, including the right to decide if, when, how much, and where they wanted to go to school, frightens and angers many people. They ask me, "Are you saying that if the parents wanted the child to go to school, and the child didn't want to go, that he wouldn't have to go? Are you saying that if the parents wanted the child to go to one school, and the child wanted to go to another, that the child would have the right to decide?" Yes, that is what I say. Some people ask, "If school wasn't compulsory, wouldn't many parents take their children out of school to exploit their labor in one way or another?" Such questions are often both snobbish and hypocritical. The questioner assumes and implies (though rarely says) that these bad parents are people poorer and less schooled than he. Also, though he appears to be defending the right of children to go to school, what he really is defending is the right of the state to compel them to go whether they want to or not. What he wants, in short, is that children should be in school, not that they should have any choice about going.

But saying that children should have the right to choose to go or not to go to school does not mean that the ideas and wishes of the parents would have no weight. Unless he is estranged from his parents and rebelling against them, a child cares very much about what they think and want. Most of the time, he doesn't want to anger or worry or disappoint them. Right now, in families where the parents feel that they have some choice about their children's schooling, there is much bargaining about schools. Such parents, when their children are little, often ask them whether they want to go to nursery school or kindergarten. Or they may take them to school for a while to try it out. Or, if they have a choice of schools, they may take them to several to see which they think they will like the best. Later, they care whether the child likes his school. If he does not, they try to do something about it, get him out of it, find a school he will like.

I know some parents who for years had a running bargain with their children, "If on a given day you just can't stand the thought of school, you don't feel well, you are afraid of something that may happen, you have something of your own that you very much want to do – well, you can stay home." Needless to say, the schools, with their supporting experts, fight it with all their might – Don't Give in to Your Child, Make Him Go to School,

He's Got to Learn. Some parents, when their own plans make it possible for them to take an interesting trip, take their children with them. They don't ask the school's permission, they just go. If the child doesn't want to make the trip and would rather stay in school, they work out a way for him to do that. Some parents, when their child is frightened, unhappy, and suffering in school, as many children are, just take him out. Hal Bennett, in his excellent book *No More Public School*, talks about ways to do this.

To say that children should have the right to control and direct their own learning, to go to school or not as they choose, does not mean that the law would forbid the parents to express an opinion or wish or strong desire on the matter. It only means that if their natural authority is not strong enough, the parents can't call in the cops to make the child do what they are not able to persuade him to do. And the law may say that there is a limit to the amount of pressure or coercion the parents can apply to the child to deny him a choice that he has a legal right to make.

When I urge that children should control their learning there is one argument that people bring up so often that I feel I must anticipate and meet it here. It says that schools are a place where children can for a while be protected against the bad influences of the world outside, particularly from its greed, dishonesty, and commercialism. It says that in school children may have a glimpse of a higher way of life, of people acting from other and better motives than greed and fear. People say, "We know that society is bad enough as it is and that children will be exposed to it and corrupted by it soon enough. But if we let children go out into the larger world as soon as they wanted, they would be tempted and corrupted just that much sooner."

They seem to believe that schools are better, more honorable places than the world outside – what a friend of mine at Harvard once called "museums of virtue." Or that people in school, both children and adults, act from higher and better motives than people outside. In this they are mistaken. There are, of course, some good schools. But on the whole, far from being the opposite of, or an antidote to, the world outside, with all its envy, fear, greed, and obsessive competitiveness, the schools are very much like it. If anything, they are worse, a terrible, abstract, simplified caricature of it. In the world outside the school, some work, at least, is done honestly and well, for its own sake, not just to get ahead of others; people are not everywhere and always being set in competition against each other; people are not (or not yet) in every minute of their lives subject to the arbitrary, irrevocable orders and judgment of others. But in most schools, a student is every minute doing what others tell him, subject to their judgment, in situations in which he can only win at the expense of other students.

This is a harsh judgment. Let me say again, as I have before, that schools are worse than most of the people in them and that many of these people do many harmful things they would rather not do, and a great many other harmful things that they do not even see as harmful. The whole of school is much worse than the sum of its parts. There are very few people in the U.S. today (or perhaps anywhere, any time) in *any* occupation, who could be trusted with the kind of power that schools give most teachers over their students. Schools seem to me among the most anti-democratic, most authoritarian, most destructive, and most dangerous institutions of modern society. No other institution does more harm or more lasting harm to more people or destroys so much of their curiosity, independence, trust, dignity, and sense of identity and worth. Even quite kindly schools are inhibited and corrupted by the knowledge of children and teachers alike that they are *performing* for the judgment and approval of others – the children for the teachers; the teachers for the parents, supervisors, school board, or the state. No one is ever free from feeling that he is being judged all the time, or soon may be. Even after the best class experiences teachers must ask themselves, "Were we right to do that? Can we prove we were right? Will it get us in trouble?"

What corrupts the school, and makes it so much worse than most of the people in it, or than they would like it to be, is its power – just as their powerlessness corrupts the students. The school is corrupted by the endless anxious demand of the parents to know how their child is doing – meaning is he ahead of the other kids – and their demand that he be kept ahead. Schools do not protect children from the badness of the world outside. They are at least as bad as the world outside, and the harm they do to the children in their power creates much of the badness of the world outside. The sickness of the modern world is in many ways a school-induced sickness. It is in school that most people learn to expect and accept that some expert can always place them in some sort of rank or hierarchy. It is in school that we meet, become used to, and learn to believe in the totally controlled society. The school is the closest we have yet been able to come to Huxley's *Brave New World*, with its alphas and betas, deltas and epsilons – and now it even has its soma. Everyone, including children, should have the right to say "No!" to it.

20
What is Unschooling?
by Earl Stevens

"What we want to see is the child in pursuit of knowledge, not knowledge in pursuit of the child." – George Bernard Shaw

It is very satisfying for parents to see their children in pursuit of knowledge. It is natural and healthy for the children, and in the first few years of life, the pursuit goes on during every waking hour. But after a few short years, most kids go to school. The schools also want to see children in pursuit of knowledge, but the schools want them to pursue mainly the school's knowledge and devote twelve years of life to doing so.

In his acceptance speech for the New York City Teacher of the Year award (1990), John Gatto said, "Schools were designed by Horace Mann... and others to be instruments of the scientific management of a mass population." In the interests of managing each generation of children, the public school curriculum has become a hopelessly flawed attempt to define education and to find a way of delivering that definition to vast numbers of children.

The traditional curriculum is based on the assumption that children must be pursued by knowledge because they will never pursue it themselves. It was no doubt noticed that, when given a choice, most children prefer not to do school work. Since, in a school, knowledge is defined as schoolwork, it is easy for educators to conclude that children don't like to acquire knowledge. Thus schooling came to be a method of controlling children and forcing them to do whatever educators decided was beneficial for them. Most children don't like textbooks, workbooks, quizzes, rote memorization, subject schedules, and lengthy periods of physical inactivity. One can discover this – even with polite and cooperative children – by asking them if they would like to add more time to their daily schedule. I feel certain that most will decline the offer.

The work of a schoolteacher is not the same as that of a homeschooling parent. In most schools, a teacher is hired to deliver a ready-made, standardized, year-long curriculum to 25 or more age-segregated children who are confined in a building all day. The teacher must use a standard curriculum – not because it is the best approach for encouraging an individual child to learn the things that need to be known – but because it is a convenient way to handle and track large numbers of children. The school curriculum is understandable only in the context of bringing administrative order out of daily chaos, of giving direction to frustrated children and unpredictable teachers. It is a system that staggers ever onward but never upward, and every morning we read about the results in our newspapers.

But despite the differences between the school environment and the home, many parents begin homeschooling under the impression that it can be pursued only by following some variation of the traditional public school curriculum in the home. Preoccupied with the idea of "equivalent education", state and local education officials assume that we must share their educational goals and that we homeschool simply because we don't want our children to be inside their buildings. Textbook and curriculum publishing companies go to great lengths to assure us that we must buy their products if we expect our children to be properly educated. As if this were not enough, there are national, state, and local support organizations that have practically adopted the use of the traditional curriculum and the school-in-the-home image of homeschooling as a *de facto* membership re-quirement. In the midst of all this, it can be difficult for a new home-schooling family to think that an alternative approach is possible.

One alternative approach is "unschooling", also known as "life learn-ing", "experience-based learning", or "independent learning". Several weeks ago, when our homeschooling support group announced a gathering to discuss unschooling, we thought a dozen or so people might attend, but more than 100 adults and children showed up. For three hours, parents and some of the children took turns talking about their homeschooling experiences and about unschooling. Many people said afterward that they left the meeting feeling reinforced and exhilarated – not because anybody told them what to do or gave them a magic formula – but because they grew more secure in making these decisions for themselves. Sharing ideas about this topic left them feeling empowered.

Before I talk about what I think unschooling is, I must talk about what it isn't. Unschooling isn't a recipe, and therefore it can't be explained in recipe terms. It is impossible to give unschooling directions for people to follow so that it can be tried for a week or so to see if it works. Unschooling isn't a method, it is a way of looking at children and at life. It is based on trust that parents and children will find the paths that work best for them – without depending on educational institutions, publishing companies, or experts to tell them what to do.

Unschooling does not mean that parents can never teach anything to their children, or that children should learn about life entirely on their own without the help and guidance of their parents. Unschooling does not mean that parents give up active participation in the education and development of their children and simply hope that something good will happen. Finally, since many unschooling families have definite plans for college, unschool-ing does not even mean that children will never take a course in any kind of a school.

Then what is unschooling? I can't speak for every person who uses the term, but I can talk about my own experiences. Our son has never had an academic lesson, has never been told to read or to learn mathematics, science, or history. Nobody has told him about phonics. He has never taken a test or been asked to study or memorize anything. When people ask, "What do you do?" My answer is that we follow our interests – and our interests inevitably lead to science, literature, history, mathematics, music – all the things that have interested people before anybody thought of them as "subjects".

A large component of unschooling is grounded in doing real things, not because we hope they will be good for us, but because they are intrinsically fascinating. There is an energy that comes from this that you can't buy with a curriculum. Children do real things all day long, and in a trusting and supportive home environment, "doing real things" invariably brings about healthy mental development and valuable knowledge. It is natural for children to read, write, play with numbers, learn about society, find out about the past, think, wonder and do all those things that society so unsuccessfully attempts to force upon them in the context of schooling.

While few of us get out of bed in the morning in the mood for a "learning experience", I hope that all of us get up feeling in the mood for life. Children always do so – unless they are ill or life has been made overly stressful or confusing for them. Sometimes the problem for the parent is that it can be difficult to determine if anything important is actually going on. It is a little like watching a garden grow. No matter how closely we examine the garden, it is difficult to verify that anything is happening at that particular moment. But as the season progresses, we can see that much has happened, quietly and naturally. Children pursue life, and in doing so, pursue knowledge. They need adults to trust in the inevitability of this very natural process, and to offer what assistance they can.

Parents come to our unschooling discussions with many questions about fulfilling state requirements. They ask: "How do unschoolers explain themselves to the state when they fill out the paperwork every year?", "If you don't use a curriculum, what do you say?" and "What about required record-keeping?" To my knowledge, unschoolers have had no problems with our state department of education over matters of this kind. This is a time when even many public school educators are moving away from the traditional curriculum, and are seeking alternatives to fragmented learning and drudgery.

When I fill out the paperwork required for homeschooling in our state, I briefly describe, in the space provided, what we are currently doing, and the general intent of what we plan to do for the coming year. I don't include long lists of books or describe any of the step-by-step skills associated with a curriculum. For example, under English/Language Arts, I mentioned that our son's favorite "subject" is the English language. I said a few words about our family library. I mentioned that our son reads a great deal and uses our computer for whatever writing he happens to do. I concluded that, "Since he already does so well on his own, we have decided not to introduce language skills as a subject to be studied. It seems to make more sense for us to leave him to his own continuing success."

Unschooling is a unique opportunity for each family to do whatever makes sense for the growth and development of their children. If we have a reason for using a curriculum and traditional school materials, we are free to use them. They are not a universally necessary or required component of unschooling, either educationally or legally.

Allowing curriculums, textbooks, and tests to be the defining, driving force behind the education of a child is a hindrance in the home as much as in the school – not only because it interferes with learning, but because it interferes with trust. As I have mentioned, even educators are beginning to question the pre-planned, year-long curriculum as an out-dated, 19th century educational system. There is no reason that families should be less flexible and innovative than schools.

Anne Sullivan, Helen Keller's mentor and friend, said:

"I am beginning to suspect all elaborate and special systems of education. They seem to me to be built upon the supposition that every child is a kind of idiot who must be taught to think. Whereas if the child is left to himself, he will think more and better, if less 'showily'. Let him come and go freely, let him touch real things and combine his impressions for himself... Teaching fills the mind with artificial associations that must be got rid of before the child can develop independent ideas out of actual experiences."

Unschooling provides a unique opportunity to step away from systems and methods, and to develop independent ideas out of actual experiences, where the child is truly in pursuit of knowledge, not the other way around.

21
Whose Goal is it, Anyway?
by Pam Laricchia

It all started with a plant. My husband was talking about training a plant – just the right combination of water and fertilizer, the right soil and sun conditions, a bit of pruning here and there, and most likely you'll be rewarded with a beautiful, healthy plant.

Like parenting, he theorized. You try to create the right environment for them, love them, nurture them, and you will likely be rewarded with successful young adults.

It sounded good, but I was having a hard time swallowing the word "training." I'm not "training" them to be anything. Training sounds like you are trying to get them to meet your goals, not their own.

"But don't you have any goals for our kids?" he asked curiously.

"No" was my short answer. But the look that flashed across his face spurred me to explain further.

"Well," I floundered, "I want them to be happy." And thinking quickly because that sounded so sappy – "I want them to be able to choose what they want to do in life and feel confident pursuing their goals."

Then I had a seemingly obvious thought: "The difference between a plant and a child is free will."

Think about it. In training a plant you are training it to your desired outcome, not the plant's. Sure, it looks "happy" on the outside – nice green leaves and bright, colorful flowers. But if the plant had free will maybe it truly would have chosen to keep that branch you trimmed off last week.

If you try to "train" a child, even in the most loving manner and with the best of intentions, you are trying to determine their goals, their path in life; you are trying to mold what they look like on the outside. And eventually that may well backfire. It will certainly take its toll on your relationship. It also manages to subvert learning about choices and goal-setting, which is so crucial in life once a person is responsible for their own actions and future.

I couldn't get the conversation out of my mind. When most people talk about goals for their kids, they usually mean things like learning to swim, being the best hockey player on the team, or getting into college – things they believe will make their kids' lives better. But whose goal is it, really? Often parents are seeing through the distortion of their own filters, not clearly through their children's eyes. It takes work to recognize and remove these filters but I have no desire to reshape my childhood by directing theirs – the risk to our relationship is too great.

In comparison, my hopes for my children aren't about accomplishments; they are about living. But I guess I do have goals for my kids! I want them to know and understand themselves. I want them to feel confident making choices. I want them to feel comfortable learning any new skills they may need to accomplish their goals. In other words, to feel confident living a joyful life. Not happy, smiley surface joy – everyone encounters disappointment and sadness – but the deep, soulful joy of being satisfied with the direction of one's life, even with its unexpected twists and turns.

So why did I choose these goals?

And how do I help my kids reach them?

To Know and Understand Themselves

I believe a strong sense of self – a deep understanding of who they are – is essential to my children confidently finding their place in our world. If they know what makes them tick, what makes their heart sing, they will be able to search for their niche, that place where they can take great pleasure in making a contribution to society. What kinds of things do they like to do? How do they like to learn? Do they like pursuing interests surrounded by others or do they prefer a more solitary approach? Do they like their activities to be predictable, or to have a sense of adventure or an element of the unknown?

Over the years they will probably realize that for many of these traits it is not one end of the spectrum or the other; they will likely find themselves enjoying elements of both to differing degrees. What is important is that they have time to discover themselves, and to realize that they are always growing, their ideas and views changing based on new facts and experiences.

Schooled children spend most of each day learning to do what other people tell them, not to mention the plethora of after-school activities and homework that fill up the remaining hours of the day. So if they don't get the time to understand themselves and discover their dreams and passions as children, they may need to take it as young adults. How often have we heard of people in their 20s going off to "find themselves"? And they are the relatively lucky ones, the ones who decide it is important to get to know themselves before they get immersed in the next stage of life – career and family. Many others just continue to pursue what they have been told will bring them happiness – the good job, the "perfect" family and so on.

Maybe they will manage to hang on for a couple more decades, though they may wear, as Dean Sluyter (Cinema Nirvana) puts it: "the drained, dispirited faces of silent adults – post-op cases who have already undergone the freedomectomy." Then the next stage of life hits and they may begin to take stock of their life so far and wonder if they are truly happy. The midlife crisis hits. "Is this really what I want to do with my life?" "Am I really happy?" Divorces and drastic career changes are all part and parcel of waiting until midlife to take the time to really know and understand yourself, what makes you tick, what brings you joy.

So, my first goal is to give our children the time and space to figure out who they truly are. And then more time and space to discover how their views evolve with age and life experience. To explore what they like to do, how they like to learn, what makes them shine. And always I am near, available to chat about what's on their mind, share my experiences or provide transportation.

I believe that giving them the time they need to understand themselves is the single most important foundation I can give them in their search for a joyful life.

To Feel Confident Making Choices

Freedom of time, so abundant in life learning, also allows our children to gain lots of experience making choices and living the outcomes. From choices as simple as what to have for breakfast, when they are tired and want to go to sleep, to bigger ones like whether to join Scouts or the local baseball league, take the time to help them figure it all out. It takes more time to give children choices – to discuss the options, the possible outcomes, time to decide which choice is best for them – than just to tell them what to do, but how else are they going to gain real experience at it? By remembering what choice you made for them last time? What will they do when they encounter a new situation and you are not right there to tell them what choice to make?

Many of us grew up that way: Our well-intentioned parents telling us what to do instead of discussing our options and ultimately letting us decide – without the guilt trip if we chose a different path. Then we may remember the heady but scary feeling of first being on our own – free to choose what to eat, what to do, to stay up all night – our time truly our own for the first time. But at that point we had moved out and had to figure it out all on our own. Which choices were truly best for us? Which were we making in reaction to our parents? Which were we making just to get along with our friends? And even with the voices in our heads (and maybe as a result of them), it took quite a while – a lot longer for some.

I don't want to be that nagging voice in my child's head as she gets older. I want to spend time with her now helping her analyze situations, possible options, likely outcomes. And supporting her decision, helping her figure out how to make choices, not what choices to make. Then when she's older that voice in her head can be her own. Though I won't mind if she occasionally hears my loving reminders that she knows what's best for her, that I trust her.

And on the other side of this coin: Children who have the freedom to try on different hats, pursue different goals and activities, and discard them when they no longer make sense, do not feel like a failure when choosing to drop something. They see it as another experience from which to learn a bit about something and a lot about themselves. This is a much better attitude than the child who is forced to stay, being told to "suck it up" and "stick it out", who feels powerless and resentful – but the lesson is learned. As an adult this child is more likely, for example, to stay in an unhappy career so as not to look or feel like a failure, though he will definitely feel trapped – not the joyful life I hope for my children.

"What work have I got to do, then?" said Will, but went on at once, "No, on second thought, don't tell me. I shall decide what I do. If you say my work is fighting, or healing, or exploring, or whatever you might say, I'll always be thinking about it. And if I do end up doing that, I'll be resentful because it'll feel as if I didn't have a choice, and if I don't do it, I'll feel guilty because I should. Whatever I do, I will choose it, no one else."

"Then you have already taken the first steps towards wisdom," said Zaphania.

This quote from *The Amber Spyglass* by Philip Pullman sums up human nature so succinctly, and describes what life learning parents are trying to do – give their children the freedom to determine their own life's journey. And through each choice made and outcome lived, our children gain experience with making choices and in turn learn a bit more about themselves. In this way my first two goals are inextricably linked, but I believe each is important enough to stand on its own.

To Feel Comfortable Learning New Skills

And my last goal is for them to feel comfortable learning new skills. It is in this area that they pick up the day-to-day skills they need to achieve their goals in life. They want to accomplish something and they are motivated to learn whatever is needed to get them there. Here they also encounter the more academic skills like reading, math and writing.

And here's another big difference between life learning and school – in school the focus is on the skills: Learning to read is in itself a goal, learning the times tables, learning the capital cities. But stuck within the confines of the school's four walls, kids find it hard to understand why they might want to learn many of these things. Those subjects are completely disconnected from the kids' goals. In school they are disconnected from life. And without the connection to real-life goals, learning these skills is all the more difficult. "Why do I need to know this?" is a common refrain, and for good reason. They need something to connect it to, some way for it to make sense in their world and with that gain understanding and real learning.

So at our house, the goal is not learning to read. But if the goal is to immerse yourself in the world of Harry Potter, you'll likely learn a lot about reading along the way. We don't have learning percentages as a goal. But if the goal is to make a well-rounded party that can defeat the final boss in your video game, an understanding of percentages and data management is pretty crucial. This learning is really incidental to the goal – just stepping stones, something to figure out along the way – but it is real learning; it makes sense in their world and has a purpose. And they truly enjoy it because it helps them accomplish their goal. Learning is fun!

I have heard people exclaim, "But what if they don't encounter a skill that they really need to know?" To which I say, "Then obviously they truly don't need it; it really wasn't necessary – yet. Or maybe ever." Without the timeline and curricula of schools there is no "start" and "end" to learning. Learning is really a byproduct of pursuing goals and interests in life – and that is a lifelong thing. There is nothing wrong with not encountering a need to learn some algebra until the age of 25. If that's when they find a use for it, that's when they can learn it! And it will make sense and be remembered because there is a real-life reason for it. Even in school, if there's no real need for a skill in a student's life (long division? historical dates? the periodic table?) they will most likely memorize it for the test and within a few weeks it is forgotten. It is questionable whether or not they actually learned or understood it at all.

So how do I help my children feel comfortable learning new things? Basically the same way I help them learn about themselves: By being there to talk to and bounce ideas off of, by sharing what I know (maybe pointing out new connections they may not have yet noticed), by helping them gather more information if they want it and by providing any "stuff" to help them pursue their interests further.

With my goal of helping my children as they learn the skills they need to pursue their goals, they are gaining experience and learning how to learn. I can't predict what they may want to learn some day, but lots of experience in figuring out how to gather information and piece it together will help them build their unique view of the world over their lifetime. It's not about telling them what to learn, but helping them figure out how to learn. As futurist Alvin Toffler put it: "The illiterate of the 21st century will not be those who cannot read and write, but those who cannot learn, unlearn and relearn."

Looking at my kids today, I tell myself that they are already living joyful lives! They do understand themselves, they are confident making their own choices (just try to convince them otherwise!) and I see them learning new things every day in pursuit of their interests and goals. Maybe my real job is to keep that spirit alive as they get older, to keep their authentic self shining brightly by protecting them from or countering those who would toss well-meaning (in their view) handfuls of sand on their soul.

It seems to me that extending life learning principles beyond academic bounds and living these goals with my children gives them a much more useful outlook on life – and a lot more self-knowledge and life skills to start with – than the one offered by school and traditional parenting practices. One that has a better chance of bringing them a joyful life. And that was my goal from the beginning.

22
Unexpected Benefits of Unschooling
by Sandra Dodd

As I write, my children are 18, 21, and 23 years old. They are in Quebec, New Mexico, and Texas. I have time to review the effects of nearly twenty years of living without school in our lives. There were some unforeseen joys, and they continue to arise.

In 1991, my firstborn child was five. His brother was three and I had just had a baby girl. My husband Keith and I started unschooling our oldest, not planning anything big or long-term. We had no fears or rancor, just thought school wouldn't be a good match for Kirby that year, with his personality.

Within months, I was confident that he wasn't going to have any problem learning if he never went to school. I had expected to see him learn the things kindergarten children learn, only in fun and creative ways. Of course, the learning happened smoothly and naturally, and didn't limit itself to anything based on age or grade level. But that's not what surprised me.

I didn't expect this to change my children's ability to make eye contact with people. It surprised me that they always had friends in such a range of ages, from younger children to young adults. Their discussions with adults were not scripted or small. They spoke directly, and kindly, with gravity or humor as the situation required.

I assumed they would be calmer and less damaged, but the extent of their self-possessed calm surpassed any imagining. They could be both sweetly childlike and truly mature all at once. It wasn't false maturity.

I didn't expect them to learn so much without me. Anyone who is involved in natural learning for any length of time can find it difficult to summarize what children have learned academically, because each child's knowledge comes from such varied sources and is fit together uniquely.

At first, though, I thought I wouldn't miss a single thing. Then I totally missed them learning Roman numerals, which they learned from the names of a series of MegaMan video games. I was jealous of that "Mega-Man" guy, at first. I felt cheated out of the fun of seeing their eyes light up. But in thinking about that feeling, I realized that if life is a busy, happy swirl, they will learn. Learning is guaranteed. The range and content will vary, but the learning will happen.

I didn't know how much people could learn without reading. As their reading ability unfolded and grew, I learned things I never knew as a teacher, and that I wouldn't have learned as an unschooling mom had they happened to have read "early." Reading is not a prerequisite for learning. Maps can be understood without knowing many words. Movies, music, museums, and TV can fill a person with visions, knowledge, experiences and connections, regardless of whether or not the person reads.

Animals respond to people the same way whether the person can read or not. People can draw and paint whether they can read or not. Non-readers can recite poetry, act in plays, learn lyrics, rhyme, play with words, and talk about all sorts of topics at length.

When school says children who can't read can't learn, what they really mean is children who can't read can't get good grades in school. Learning is quite a different thing, as it turns out!

I didn't expect my children to be offered jobs they didn't even apply for. I know it doesn't happen with everyone, but there are other life learners, too, who have found that being around a wide range of people and being involved in a variety of activities has brought opportunities to show responsibility and helpful energy even at a young age. Each of my children had opportunities to do meaningful work in their mid-teens, at jobs in which there were things to learn.

Kirby was offered a job in a gaming store when he turned fourteen. They hired him to run the Saturday morning *Pokémon* league, and gradually increased his hours. When he was sixteen, he was legally able to open and close, so he had keys to the store. They would send him to *Magic the Gathering* tournaments to represent the shop (sell supplies) or to judge the games.

Marty, our second son, was offered a job at fifteen, helping make boots and leather bags for historical re-enactors. He worked there for over a year and learned a great deal. Part of the training was to make a pair of boots for himself and to wear them, so he knew what they felt like and what could go wrong. He still has those boots, and re-soled them himself.

At fifteen and sixteen, Holly babysat the children of an unschooling mom in grad school for a while. She stayed at their home and took care of the house, kids and dogs, and took the girls places outside the house, too.

All three of my teenaged offspring subsequently had jobs they applied for: phone tech support, grocery store, flower shop, skateboard shop, pizza parlor, Persian restaurant. Having had a job before was helpful in each case. Most of those jobs lasted over a year. When they moved on, the owners were always sorry to see them go.

I didn't know that our relationships could stay so good even when they were teenagers. My original expectation was that when they were teens they would be frustrated and rebellious and wild, because I thought that was hormonally inevitable.

A side benefit of having been partners rather than adversaries was that the "normal teen behavior" turned out not to have been "natural," and in contrast to what I was seeing in unschooled teens, it started to look like very sensible reactions to a barrage of arbitrary rules and limitations. The communications and trust continued to build within our family, rather than to erode over the years.

I didn't know they would be so compassionate and courageous. Partly, they weren't taught to be cold and mean by school prejudices, cliques, bullies, and impatient teachers. Looking back at my own childhood, the things I regret having done were nearly always instigated by a friend in school. And I was a pretty strong-willed kid.

Partly, they have had a gentle life, and harshness surprised them when they saw it.

I've heard stories from all of them, and sometimes seen myself, that they would physically and verbally assist other children who were afraid or feeling embarrassed. It happened in homes, parks, fast-food playgrounds, and as they got older it happened at campouts, and parties, and walking around in public.

Marty broke off a friendship when he was nine, because he didn't like the way the friend treated the younger brother when Marty was visiting. Marty played with the younger brother too, and wanted to include him, but it just made the older boy even more cruel to his brother. As a younger brother himself, Marty was unwillingly to be a catalyst for the situation, and stopped visiting.

Some of the stories involved asking an adult to act differently. That felt very brave to me, because of the way I grew up. But my children saw it as assisting another child, not as "talking back" to or challenging an adult. I was impressed at what seemed like courage to me but was normal behavior for them.

I didn't expect to like to lose arguments. I enjoy it when my kids win an argument with me or Keith. We've laughed about that later when we're alone. Keith used to be bothered by it when they were little. At first, he was surprised each time he saw them arguing, thinking they should be more respectful of my stated opinions or suggestions. I told him I figured if they could win arguments with me, they'd do okay for themselves out in the world. That made sense to him, so he started willingly engaging them in "yeah, but…" kinds of discussions, and as time passed we all got better at it and clearer about our priorities. We knew each other better, too, and had more knowledge of and respect for the intellectual abilities of everyone in the family.

I didn't know I would be so accepting of kids saying "no." We have a large, funky piece of furniture Keith built years ago – a corner shelf with three electrical outlets built in. It needed to be moved, and we were considering taking it to the dump.

As I was unloading my sewing supplies and cloth from that onto a new shelf, I became nostalgic. It's big and bulky, but it used to be our stereo shelf, and held the turntable and speakers and tapes. And it would hold Marty's TV and Playstation, I thought. And Marty had been talking about getting an old couch out of his room.

We asked Marty if he wanted it. He did.

"Now?"

"Not right now."

Oh. He can take it in a few days.

Marty had good reasons to wait and we were just as calm with a kid saying "wait" as we would've been with one of us saying it to the other adult partner.

I think most parents would have said, "No, we're doing it now; stop what you're doing, cancel your plans for tomorrow, it's our house…" and by all that the furniture would've been imbued with sorrow and frustration. The parents would have thought less of the kid, the kid thought less of the parents, and so in on several directions. But we really listened to Marty. We knew him well enough to know he was making a thoughtful, honest decision. It's hard not to respect that.

I didn't expect it to make things so sweet between me and Keith. Partly Keith is just a nice guy, but principles that applied to the kids applied to the adults, too, and we all experienced and shared more patience and understanding.

Being compassionate about kids' changes helped us respond to our own and each others' needs and changes.

The first time Kirby saw me, the day he was born, he gave me a look Keith had been giving me for eight years already, that I used to interpret as "a dirty look." After I saw it on Kirby, I stopped thinking it was mean and personal when I saw it on my husband. It was a thoughtful look.

The more I got to know Marty, the more I saw his genetic similarities to his dad, and because I was sympathetic to those traits in Marty which had bothered me in Keith, I became more sympathetic and understanding of Keith. Also, because Marty and Keith were so similar, I started seeing how different Keith might have been if his parents hadn't been less strict and more attentive.

Keith and I have been together for thirty-two years and married for twenty-six years. One of the things that strengthened our relationship was the personal satisfaction of seeing that together we had brought up some really great kids, by being steadfast and courageous even though friends and relatives sometimes thought we had no idea what we were doing and should put those kids in school.

I didn't expect unschooling to make the grocery store so fun. When I had babies and toddlers, the store was like a museum. We could go slowly and look at things we didn't even intend to buy. We would weigh things, just to use the scales. Sometimes I took two carts – one for the baby and the groceries, and one for the younger kids. I would push one and pull the other, and we would talk, plan the day, and tell stories.

When Holly was fourteen or so, a grocery store just a few hundred yards out our back gate had a grand opening. I didn't know there would be a ribbon-cutting, or we would have gone a little bit earlier. We did see the giant scissors and the leftover ribbon, and the podium where the speech had been made. She was the only teen there, as it was a weekday morning.

There was live music (classical guitarist doing some local music, and some jazz and pop too). There was a big "congratulations" cake. There were flowers being handed out. The store was perfect. Everything was amazingly arranged, and when I told the manager how beautiful the produce was and that I thought nobody would buy any today because nobody would want to mess it up, he laughed and admitted it was pretty wonderful. He said it took eight people to do that, and even the green beans were laid in individually. I was talking about the peppers, which were clearly laid in as people do mortarless stonework, taking the shape of each pepper into consideration.

Everyone was being nice to everyone else even though it was crowded and the carts were nearly all being used. The kids we saw besides Holly were very young. Strangers were cooing over babies, and oohing over the beauty of the inner remodeling done on that old building. Flagstone columns. Mexican tile. It was as exciting a trip to a grocery store as I will ever hope for.

Holly went to the store hungry, and of all the foods in the world she could bring back for breakfast she wanted microwaveable pizza. Although I tried to talk her into fresh orange sweet rolls or donuts from the new bakery, she said (in front of two older women who were listening to the whole conversation), "No, I don't want anything sweet. I just want the pizza."

I didn't expect to see school so differently. "School is what you make of it," they used to say. I can see some possibilities in that, but school is only so soft, and only so safe. What I made of it, when I was a kid, was a contest. I usually won easily. I didn't expect my ongoing review of school to make me wish I had not walked through those races. I wish other kids had won more. Part of that is free-floating guilt and shame. My success created someone else's failure, because schools are competitive in many different ways.

I didn't expect unschooling to create a shameless life, but one day I said to Holly, jokingly, "Aren't you ashamed?" As verbal as she is, that was a new word to her. She didn't know what "ashamed" meant. She was twelve or thirteen.

When I was young, people used to say, "You should be ashamed" to each other, and to me, and around me. And I was ashamed – I just hadn't found the reason for it yet. Shame is like an indwelling virus that surfaces when we're weak, once it's in there.

I didn't know that people could grow up without having a wad of shame inside them, waiting to surface. Then I saw my children grow up, whole and strong and not ashamed.

I didn't expect this to improve my relationships with pets. I noticed one morning that I was really patient with my irritating cat. We've long been sweeter with our current dog than we ever were with a dog before, and somewhat the cats too, but usually I hiss at the cat to get away from me when he gets in my face early in the morning and this morning I told myself that the cat can't open a can, and he's excited that I'm awake, and the dog probably ate their canned food, so I just very calmly followed him in there and fed him and he was very happy. I doubt it's my last frontier; it's just a recent frontier.

We leave food down for our dog. A favorite neighbor dog used to come in and have some. When a friend house-sat for us, she was surprised that our dog and cats didn't mind her dog eating from their dishes. Usually, her dog is fed separately, and finishes it all immediately. Ours know there will be some more later, so they only eat when they're hungry.

I didn't know it would affect the way I care for my yard. I successfully grew moonflowers, which bloomed at night. Many sources recommended nicking the seeds. I soaked them instead, and they sprouted and grew beautifully. Nicking the seeds sounded like something very likely to go against Nature. How did I know which part of the seed was cuttable? My boys weren't circumcised, and I didn't nick my seeds.

A good analogy for helping children grow in their own ways is the growth of trees from seed. An apple seed cannot grow an oak tree. Each seed has within it all it needs to know what kind of roots and leaves it will make. What young trees need is good soil, enough water, and protection from damage.

We have trees I planted from seed. They're as tall as my house. I would not have thought I would have the patience for that, but something changed. I decided all I would do would be to collect the seeds, one day when we were at a homeschool gathering at a park. Then I thought I would just see if they would sprout. Some did.

I wondered what the baby trees would look like. They grew. I transplanted them into the yard after a couple of years, accepting that they might perish. They lived.

I was a little surprised to find out how much of unschooling is doing, rather than just not doing. Unschoolers are not sitting in the back corner of the homeschooling world doing nothing. We're doing something profound and direct.

Unschoolers have experiences other homeschoolers don't have. Unschoolers know things that teachers cannot learn in or around school.

Unschoolers who start early enough can have relationships with their children for which there are hardly any words.

I have no sons- or daughters-in-law yet. I have no grandchildren. I'm not through learning how my children's lives will turn out. At some point, I won't be there to witness it anymore, but I'm happier with the outcome than I ever imagined I could have been when we started.

23
Grown Without Schooling
by Jason Hunt

This interview was given to five unschoolers for a feature story in the Spring 2010 issue of German magazine Unerzogen.

What are your current interests and plans for the future (that's what interests most people – will they be able to make a career)? Are you going to study something and get an official degree? So far, I've developed and maintained our website at naturalchild.org, edited and laid out books, and have my own business fixing computers and giving technical support, all things I've learned on my own, and continue to develop. As for what else I might do in the future, I don't know. I don't see why I couldn't study something "officially" if I felt I would benefit from it. Then again, as I find time to try new things, I think I'm personally inclined to explore more creative endeavors, like writing or graphic art, that I can learn in my own way, at my own pace, and on my own terms.

What's your greatest passion? Do you live it, or are there any obstacles you have yet to overcome? I have many interests – computers and technology, graphic art, exploring nature, I'm a movie buff... I don't really have a "great passion." I see life as more of an adventure than a pre-set path to one particular goal.

What does the term "unschooling" mean to you? (I know there are some people out there who would consider themselves unschoolers who aren't half as "radical" as we are, hence the question). It means rejecting everything the school system tells us about learning. Not creating a class-room at home. Not using grades, assignments, or tests. It means answering questions, making information available. It means trusting children to learn, and throwing out the absurd notion that we have to force them to learn – a notion that actually does more harm to the learning process than anything. We've evolved to have an instinctual drive to learn what we need to know to be a part of our society. No one is more curious than a child before they go to school. They want to know everything – until school con-vinces them that learning must not be fun – otherwise, why would they have to be forced to do it?

Was it your decision to leave school at some point, or did you unschool from the start (i.e. were your parents already weirdos)? Oh yeah, they're weirdos... but that had nothing to do with it! I think they were just fortunate to read the right things, like John Holt's books and Growing Without Schooling, and found support from other families. I unschooled from the beginning.

Do you feel you are lacking anything compared to former schooled kids? No.

Can you do math? Math has always been one of my favorite topics. I have just about every book by Martin Gardner – he presents serious math in a fun and interesting way – often in the form of puzzles, games and ex-periments, that really make you understand the underlying concepts. An-other similar, great book is *Mathematics: A Human Endeavor* by Harold Jacobs. The tag line of that one is "A book for those who think they don't like the subject." It's full of humor, and explains everything in plain, friend-ly English.

Do you feel your life as a kid has been better than the lives of the school kids you knew? If so, how? I'm very grateful for the childhood I was able to have. My time has been my own. Being in charge of my own life, what I learn about, how, and when... I can't imagine it any other way.

Do you feel your life now is better than the lives of many former school kids around you? If so, how? It's difficult to know what's due to unschooling or not, since I've never known any other way, but I feel like I still have that same curiosity and wonder as when I was a child. I still love learning new things, and always will. I feel like my attitudes and ideals are completely self-developed, and I think I've been able to avoid, to some extent, some of the silly things in our culture – materialism, conformity, predefined notions of success (things that I think may be largely created by, and propagated by, school). Maybe this is just who I am, but I've always been allowed to be exactly who I am.

If you have or want to have children – are they/will they be unschoolers? They would definitely be unschooled – no question. Of course they would have a choice – but who would choose to go to school?

And here comes another classic: Do you feel that you and your parents are too close so that it hinders you (or them) in your personal development? On the contrary, it's been a source of strength. I've always had a great relationship with my parents. We're friends, and equals. We live together, work together, and have fun together. But we have our own lives too.

Are your parents key figures of the unschooling scene, and how did that influence you? My mother (Jan Hunt) has been writing about parenting and unschooling... well, for as long as I can remember. The way it influenced me was to make me want to do all I could to help – by creating her website, editing articles and books – we recently published a collection of unschooling stories and articles called *The Unschooling Unmanual* – all of which I learned to do by doing it. I just want to do whatever I can to help get the word out, so as many children as possible can have what I had.

Is your world view very similar or rather different from your parents'
world views? Our philosophy is pretty similar – in broad terms, valuing all
people, and believing we should all help each other. In terms of how we
think, I'm the most scientifically-minded one. I believe in logic, skepticism,
and reason. I think this way all the time, but it comes in quite handy when
fixing computers – I enjoy the detective-work element of it; whatever's going on, there's a cause – it's a matter of theory, experiment, trial and error.
Just like how learning works.

Unschooling Resources

Books

How Children Learn, by John Holt

"This enduring classic of educational thought offers teachers and parents deep, original insight into the nature of early learning. John Holt was the first to make clear that, for small children, 'learning is as natural as breathing.' In this delightful yet profound book, he looks at how we learn to talk, to read, to count, and to reason, and how we can nurture and encourage these natural abilities in our children." (Amazon.com)

The Unschooling Handbook, by Mary Griffith

"Did you know that a growing percentage of home schoolers are becoming unschoolers? The unschooling movement is founded on the principle that children learn best when they pursue their own natural curiosities and interests. Without bells, schedules, and rules about what to do and when, the knowledge they gain through mindful living and exploration is absorbed more easily and enthusiastically. Learning is a natural, inborn impulse, and the world is rich with lessons to be learned and puzzles to be solved. Successful unschooling parents know how to stimulate and direct their children's learning impulse. Once you read this book, so will you!" (Amazon.com)

Life Learning, edited by Wendy Priesnitz

"Academics, parents and young people describe why non-compulsory, non-coercive, active, respectful, interest-led, family- and community-based learning from life is growing in popularity and will displace prescribed curriculum, standardized testing and the other regurgitation-based relics of our outmoded school system. This innovative way of learning through living not only fosters intellectual development and academic achievement, it allows children and young people to develop an understanding of themselves and their place in modern society so they can create a better world." (NaturalLifeBooks.com)

Weapons of Mass Instruction, by John Taylor Gatto

"John Taylor Gatto's *Weapons of Mass Instruction* focuses on mechanisms of traditional education that cripple imagination, discourage critical thinking, and create a false view of learning as a byproduct of rote-memorization drills. Gatto demonstrates that the harm school inflicts is rational and deliberate. The real function of pedagogy, he argues, is to render the common population manageable. To that end, young people must be conditioned to rely upon experts, to remain divided from natural alliances, and to accept disconnections from their own lived experiences. They must at all costs be discouraged from developing self-reliance and independence. Escaping this trap requires strategy that Gatto calls 'open source learning' which imposes no artificial divisions between learning and life. Through this alternative approach, our children can avoid being indoctrinated – only then can they achieve self-knowledge, judgment, and courage."
(Amazon.com)

Education: Free & Compulsory, by Murray Rothbard

"In this radical and scholarly monograph, Murray N. Rothbard identifies the crucial feature of our educational system that dooms it to fail: at every level, from financing to attendance, the system relies on compulsion instead of voluntary consent. Certain consequences follow. The curriculum is politicized to reflect the ideological priorities of the regime in power. Standards are continually dumbed down to accommodate the least common denominator. The brightest children are not permitted to achieve their potential, the special-needs of individual children are neglected, and the mid-level learners become little more than cogs in a machine. The teachers themselves are hamstrung by a political apparatus that watches their every move. Rothbard explores the history of compulsory schooling to show that none of this is by accident. The state has long used compulsory schooling, backed by egalitarian ideology, as a means of citizen control. An interesting feature of this book is its promotion of individual, or home, schooling, long before the current popularity of the practice."
(Amazon.com)

Parenting a Free Child, by Rue Kream

"How do the principles of unschooling apply to television viewing, toothbrushing, and chores? How can we develop respectful relationships with our children? How do unschooled children learn to read? *Parenting A Free Child* addresses these issues and more in an easily accessible question and answer format." (Amazon.com)

The Unschooling Unmanual, edited by Jan & Jason Hunt

This books features 11 essays by 8 writers on living and learning naturally, lovingly, and respectfully.

Websites

SandraDodd.com is home to one of the most influential unschoolers in the world, Sandra Dodd. Her website is a large, and growing, collection of unschooling and parenting wisdom from decades of experience, both her own and others. From the site, "Learning for fun is the most fun way to learn, and to live. I have gathered much and written some to inspire you to revel in your own learning, in your children's learning, and in your friends' curiosity and happiness in the face of a world of information!"

LifeLearningMagazine.com will "help you discover how to employ self-directed, life-based learning in your own life and/or that of your child. Read all about how other people just like you and your children have learned without being taught... what helps and what hinders, and what they have achieved in their lives as a result. Laugh, cry and identify with parents who are helping themselves and their children learn from the real world... and learning a lot about themselves along the way. Think about how we are limited by a society that believes in coercive education... and how we can transcend those limits in our daily lives. Find support and reassurance for interest-based, learner-directed education (for all ages) and non-coercive, natural parenting."

Unschoolers.com is a "a website dedicated to providing detailed and helpful information on everything related to unschooling and home-schooling. You'll find local support group listings, news, articles, book recommendations, and links."

Radical Unschooling Info is a Facebook group dedicated to supporting unschoolers throughout their journey. With over a thousand members, unschoolers new and old help each other navigate the wonderful world of unschooling and peaceful parenting.

Found at http://www.facebook.com/groups/303347574750.

FamilyRUN.ning.com is home to the Radical Unschoolers Network, where radical unschooling families and those interested in radical unschooling can share experiences, plan events, and learn more about radical unschooling.

Section Five – Parenting

24
Natural Born Bullies
by Robin Grille

The media attention given recently to the phenomenon of bullying in schools, is truly a cause for celebration. Finally our world has begun to take seriously the plight of children: the most powerless sector of the community. Initiatives under way in schools are designed to intervene by identifying bullies and their victims, and then providing counseling and education in more effective social skills. Programs have been developed to teach school bullies alternative behaviors, impulse control, conflict resolution and negotiation skills. The victims of bullying are offered support, protection, and trained in assertiveness wherever practicable.

Though this allopathic approach may yield some benefits, the problem with it is that it's only a partial solution. If in our attempts to eliminate violence from schools, we narrow our focus to treating the bully, we might be presuming that he or she is the "bad child", sole originator of the violence. It is all too easy and very tempting to blame bullies for their bullying behavior. We single them out, brand them as "behavioral problem child", or perhaps attention deficit child. The odds are that someone in a laboratory somewhere is trying to isolate a "bullying" gene. There's even bound to be a pharmaceutical company searching for a biochemical cause of bullying: "wait till our shareholders hear we have developed a pacifying drug for bul-ly-children!"

When we ask a child who is hurting to bear all of the responsibility for their aggressive behavior, we have in a way retaliated by bullying the bully. This in fact adds up to ignoring that a bully is in pain, they have been hurt in some way and are acting out their hurt on others. The truth is that violence does not sprout from within individuals, it is a symptom of families that are hurting, perhaps with members that are hurting each other.

If we believe that better social interaction skills can be learned, by implication we must also believe that violent tendencies are also learned. This will be irksome to those who cherish the idea of an "evil" nature that people are just born with. A prodigious number of studies, replicated worldwide, have shown that violence in the home (both physical and verbal) produces violent children. In Australian research, a link was found between family dysfunction and violent children (Rigby K, *Journal of Family Therapy*, May 1994)*. Few notions are so well supported by the research literature, yet it's surprising how little attention is given to the families of bullies.

Bullying is best understood as an adaptive behavior that makes sense within certain family environments. A study by Baldry A.C. and Farrington D.P. published in the *Journal of Legal and Criminological Psychology* (September 1998) examined 11-14 year old school children who reported being bullies and/or victims. Both types of children were found to come from homes where "authoritarian" styles of parenting were employed. In other words: "you'll do as you're told, or else, no questions asked!". Author-itarian parenting is characterized by punitiveness, an immutable power imbalance which favors the parents, and an absence of explanation, nego-tiation, or consultation.

Social Learning Theory is a mainstream school of psychological thought which states that violent behavior is brought about through learn-

---

* For references, see: http://goo.gl/an58H

ing. Supported by an enormous body of research data, Social Learning advocates explain that children learn to be violent chiefly through imitation of violent role models. This means that parents who rely on corporal punishment or verbal abuse to "control" their kids are unwittingly acting as models for bullying behavior (Bandura 1973, Baron, 1977). Secondary sources of modeled violence include older siblings, media violence, peers and even school teachers. Spatz-Widom (1989) conducted an exhaustive analysis of research addressing whether violence is trans-generational. She found substantial support for the notion that violence is begotten by violence. Few things are so well agreed upon by psychologists across the board. This relationship holds true even for verbal violence, as researchers Vissing Y.M. *et al* (journal article in *Child Abuse and Neglect*, 1991) found. Their study revealed that children who had experienced higher levels of verbal aggression at home (being sworn at or insulted) exhibited higher rates of delinquency and interpersonal aggression.

The list goes on, *ad infinitum*, with studies such as: McCord's (1979) study of 230 boys, which found that he was able to accurately predict criminal behavior based on violent upbringing in 3/4 of cases. Sheline *et al* (1994) found that elementary school boys' "behavior problems" were consistently traceable to lack of parental affection, and to parental use of spanking for discipline. In a study of 570 German families, Muller *et al* (1995) found a direct path between harsh punishment and anti-social behavior in children.

Recently, psychologist Elizabeth Gershoff (2002) undertook the mammoth task of collecting all studies done in over 60 years to investigate the effects of corporal punishment – 88 studies in all. She only considered studies looking at ordinary smacking or spanking, and excluded any that looked at physically injurious or legally abusive punishment. The evidence she found was consistent across all studies, and overwhelming: even ordinary smacking tends to make children more aggressive. We can no longer pretend to ourselves that ordinary smacking is not a form of violence, since it can – and often does – lead to more aggressive attitudes in children.

It is not too difficult to understand why children who are punished physically can become bullies. As far back as 1977, research psychologists Walters and Grusec concluded: "that physical punishment... leads to an increase in aggressive behavior, and that the mechanism for this increase is imitation." The smacking or spanking parent is unwittingly acting as a role-model for aggressive behavior. The way this works was ingeniously demonstrated by a series of experiments reported in Bandura's 1973 book *Aggression: A Social Learning Analysis*. These experiments graphically depicted the way children would imitate adults who acted violently toward toy dummies.

For role-modeled behavior to be efficiently transmitted, three main conditions must be met. Firstly, children are more likely to imitate role models that they look up to or love. That's why parents are such powerful role models. Secondly, the role model's actions are more likely to be imitated if they are seen to meet with success. In other words, the attitude that "might is right" is passed on when a spanking disciplinarian succeeds in changing a child's behavior, and remains unchallenged. The third condition is that violence must be legitimized and sanctioned in order to be imitated. In other words, children more readily adopt violent attitudes if they have been made to believe that harsh punishment is "deserved".

It's been shown that violent children come from violent or neglectful homes. This matter has been put to rest. But only about half of abused children grow up to be abusive. Why? Individuals who remain convinced that verbal or physical assaults against them were "deserved" are significantly more likely to act out violently. This is also true for violence witnessed against others. Bandura (1973) refers to a study that found that children displayed much more imitation of violent behaviors depicted on video, if these behaviors were approved by an adult, less so if the adult was silent, and even less if the adult expressed disapproval of the video violence. Children who grow up believing that being hit is what they well-deserved, go on to be more accepting of and de-sensitized to violence in general. They are candidates for the ranks of bullies, victims, or both.

A side-effect of harsh punishment is that it de-sensitizes people to their pain, then also to the pain of others. This de-sensitization process is what facilitates the acting out of violence. The process of de-sensitization to violence begins when a child who, branded as "bad" or "naughty", accepts the blame and the assault that comes with it. A "tough skin" grows over the wound, which obscures the depth of the pain that throbs beneath. The pain and betrayal felt is sealed off, minimized, trivialized, or denied. Deafness to one's own pain entails indifference to the pain of others. Those whose anger boils over become bullies, those who are paralyzed with fear, the victims. Others hover in between, harboring a predilection to retributional and "might is right" attitudes. The landscape is dotted with the punished and the beaten; who grow up to make light of it, or to stoically profess that, "it never did me any harm!".

How grossly adults tend to dilute or whitewash any violence they suffered as children, is grimly illustrated by studies such as that of Berger *et al* (1988) and Knutson and Selner (1994). Both studies found numerous respondents who reported having been punished in their childhood so brutally as to require hospitalization, but only 43% and 60% (respectively) of these considered themselves abused! By contrast, Hunter and Kilstrom (1979) found that people who were openly angry about any abuse they had suffered as children, were statistically less likely to transmit this abuse onto others. Beaten children who are at risk of becoming bullies or offenders can be helped once somebody can make it abundantly clear to them that spankings or thrashings are not just nor deserved.

A wholistic and therefore more effective approach to "treating" school bullies would be to compassionately examine the environment in which the violent responses were learned, and then to work cooperatively with family members to alter the dynamics of this environment. If violence is an adaptive behavior learned within a family system, it makes no sense to teach a bully not to be violent, only to send him or her back to the original system that they are powerless to change. It must be understood that bullying behavior is a reaction to powerlessness. To consider bullies as offenders is superficial, when in fact, they are victims. The fundamental way in which the family operates must change, through exposure to alternative means to authoritarian, punitive or "power-over" methods of child-control.

Systems-theory based family therapy models are non-blaming, they recognize and affirm that each family member is doing their best given the resources available to them. New options for more enhancing ways to interact can be taught, without finding fault in any individual. Why not have a policy that makes it standard procedure to invite parents or carers of school bullies to the school? The purpose would be to identify any areas where parents might need support through stressful situations, to train parents in assertive and non-authoritarian parenting methods, and to empower parents by including them cooperatively in programs to assist their children.

As long as any kind of violence is sanctioned in the home, there will be bullies. Bullies in schools, bullies in business, bullies in politics. There will also be victims. This is not a fact of life, but an artifact of history. Historians and anthropologists have only recently discovered that, up until very recently, and for most of human history, child-rearing has tended to be extremely violent (de Mause 1982 and 1988, Blaffer-Hrdy 2001, Boswell 1988). It is no wonder that violence persists in so many forms, across all age groups, and that most of us are capable of slipping and treating our children violently on occasions, even if we strive against it.

The good news is that the beating, spanking and verbal abuse of children is on its way out, as an overall world trend. So far, over ten countries have legislated against corporal punishment in the home, many more are in the process of doing so, and over 120 countries have banned it from their schools. A survey by Gelles & Straus (*Journal of Interpersonal Violence*, June 1987) found that although there still is an extremely high incidence of violence against children in the USA, it had decreased from 1975 to 1985 by a factor of 47%. By millennium's end, the approval of any kind of corporal punishment by American parents had fallen to little more than half of respondents. Trends such as these are cause for optimism that bullying will become a rarer phenomenon. This progress will accelerate if we keep remembering that every bully we meet is someone who is being or has been bullied; if we endeavor to treat the system rather than the symptom.

25
Childhood: The Unexplored Source of Knowledge
by Alice Miller

Probably ever since civilization began, people have been debating about how Evil came into the world and what we can do to combat it. There has always been a diffuse intuitive conviction that the seeds of Evil are to be sought in childhood, but the ruling tendency has been to imagine it as something congenital, the manifestation of innate destructive instincts best transformed into goodness, decency, and nobility of character by a liberal dose of corporal punishment.

This is a position that is still frequently championed. Today, no one seriously believes that the Devil has a hand in things, smuggling some changeling into the cradle and forcing us to employ strict upbringing methods to batter this diabolical offspring into submission. But from some quarters we do hear the serious contention that there are such things as genes that predispose certain individuals to delinquency. The quest for these rogue genes has inspired many a respectable research project, even though the hypotheses behind it fly in the face of a number of proven facts. Advocates of the "congenital evil" theory would, for example, have to explain why, 30 to 40 years before the Third Reich reared its ugly head, there was such a sudden spate of children with "bad genes" ready at a later date to do Hitler's bidding with such alacrity.

Sufficient scientific evidence has been marshaled to refute the notion that some people are just "born bad." This absurd myth, encountered in almost all cultures, has been effectively exploded. It is dead, but it refuses to lie down. We know today that the brain we are born with is not the finished product it was once thought to be. The structuring of the brain depends very much on experiences gone through in the first hours, days and weeks of a person's life. The stimulus indispensable for developing the capacity for empathy, say, is the experience of loving care. In the absence of such care, when a child is forced to grow up neglected, emotionally starved, and subjected to physical cruelty, he or she will forfeit this innate capacity.

Of course we do not arrive in this world as a clean slate. Every new baby comes with a history of its own, the history of the nine months between conception and birth. In addition, children have the genetic blueprint they inherit from their parents. These factors may determine what kind of a temperament a child will have, what inclinations, gifts, pre-dispositions. But character depends crucially upon whether a person is given love, protection, tenderness and understanding in the early formative years or exposed to rejection, coldness, indifference, cruelty. The number of children committing murders is on the increase, and very many of them were born to adolescent, drug-dependent mothers. Extreme neglect, lack of attachment, and traumatization are the rule in such cases.

In the last few years, neuro-biologists have further established that traumatized and neglected children display severe lesions affecting anything up to 30% of those areas of the brain that control our emotions. Severe traumas inflicted on infants lead to an increase in the release of stress hormones that destroy the existing, newly formed neurons and their interconnections.

More than anyone else, the credit for recognizing the immense import of these discoveries for our understanding of infant development and the delayed effects of traumas and neglect must go to neurologist and child psychiatrist Dr. Bruce D. Perry. His studies confirm what I described in my book *For Your Own Good* 20 years ago as a result of observing my patients and studying educational literature. In that work I quoted extensively from the manuals of what I have called the poisonous pedagogy with their insistence on the importance of drumming the principles of obedience and cleanliness into babies in the very first days and weeks of their existence. Studying this literature helped me to understand what made it possible for individuals such as Adolf Eichmann to function like killer robots without even the slightest stirrings of compunction. The people who turned into Hitler's willing executioners had accounts to settle that dated back to their earliest days. They were people who had never been given the opportunity for an adequate response to the extreme cruelty inflicted on them in infancy. Their latent destructive potential was not the product of some Freudian "death drive" but the early suppression of natural reactions.

The fact that the monstrous advice about "good" parenting disseminated by self-styled educationalists in Germany around 1860 went into as many as 40 editions led me to conclude that most parents had read them and did indeed act – in good faith – on the recommendations set out there. They beat their children from the outset because they had been told this was the way to make decent members of society out of them. 40 years later, the children thus treated did the same with their children. They didn't know any better. Born 30 to 40 years before the Holocaust, those traumatized children later became Hitler's adherents, adulators, and henchmen. In my view, it was the direct result of their early drilling. The cruelty they experienced turned them into emotional cripples incapable of developing any kind of empathy for the sufferings of others. At the same time it made them into people living with a time-bomb, unconsciously waiting for an opportunity of venting on others the rage pent up inside them. Hitler gave them the legal scapegoat they needed to acting out their early feelings and their thirst for vengeance.

The latest discoveries about the human brain might have been expected to bring about a radical change in our thinking about children and the way we treat them. But as we know only too well, old habits die hard. It takes at least two generations for young parents to free themselves of the burden of inherited "wisdom" and stop beating their own children, two generations until it has become impossible to give one's child a slap "inadvertently", two generations before the weight of newly acquired knowledge gets in the way of the hand raised to deal the "unthinking" blow.

Alongside the habits stored in our bodies and favoring misguided behavior, there are also a host of opinions still passionately advocated by experts although they are demonstrably false. One of these is the belief that in the long run the effects of corporal punishment are salutary rather than detrimental. Such opinions can only be espoused by completely ignoring the childhood factor and its effects on the later development of individuals. As the experts in question inherited these opinions from their parents when they were children themselves, their belief in them prevails over all the weight of scientific evidence pointing to the contrary.

These thoughts, which I have set out in much greater detail in my latest book *Paths of Life*, will perhaps suffice to suggest the immense significance I ascribe to the experiences undergone by infants in the first days, weeks and months of their lives to explain their later behavior. In no way do I wish to assert that later influences are completely ineffectual. On the contrary. For a traumatized or neglected child it is of crucial importance to encounter what I call a "helping" or a "knowing witness" in its immediate circle. But such witnesses can only really help if they are aware of the consequences of early deprivations and do not play them down. It is in disseminating the information required by such potential knowing witnesses that I see my prime mission.

For a long time, the significance of the first few months of life for the later adult was a neglected subject even among psychologists. In several of my books I have tried to cast some light on this area by discussing the biographies of dictators like Hitler, Stalin, Ceaucescu and Mao and demonstrating how they unconsciously reenacted their childhood situation on the political stage. Here, however, I want to turn my attention away from history and the past and train my gaze on our present practice. My conviction is that in numerous areas of practical life we could be more productive if we paid the childhood factor greater heed than is customarily the case. Here are some examples.

The area in which the willful neglect of the childhood factor is most apparent is, so it seems to me, the penal system. Statistics tell us that 90% of the prisoners in American jails were abused in childhood. This figure is astonishingly high if we bear in mind the denial and repression factor. Probably the real figure is closer to a full 100%. A sheltered and respected child does not turn criminal. But most delinquents deny the sufferings they went through as a child. Despite that, we still have this high – and highly eloquent – figure. Unfortunately little has been done to integrate this knowledge into the way prisons are organized and run. Outwardly, of course, today's prisons and penitentiaries have little in common with the grim fortresses of the 19th century. But one thing has stayed much the same: questions like what made an individual prisoner a criminal in the first place, what features of his early life set him off in that direction, and what he could do to avoid falling into the same trap over and over again are very rarely posed. In order to answer these questions himself, the prisoner would have to be encouraged to talk, write and think about his life as a child and share these facts with others in a structured group setting.

In my latest book I report on a program of this nature in Canada. Thanks to group work, a number of fathers who had sexually abused their daughters understood for the first time that their actions were criminal. Of crucial importance for them was that they were able to talk about their childhood to other people they trusted. That way they learned to grasp how they had automatically passed on something they had experienced themselves without realizing it.

We are accustomed not to say anything about the things we have suffered in childhood and frequently, instead of saying anything, we act blindly instead. But it was precisely the opportunity for talking about these things that released these prisoners from their blindness, gave them access to heightened awareness and protected them from acting out. Programs like these are unfortunately still very much the exception. The only other one I know of is at a prison in Arizona where violent criminals can talk about their childhood and with the help of the group learn to decipher the covert meaning in their life histories. I have seen video recordings of these group sessions and I was impressed by the change in the facial expressions of these men after therapy. Proceeding in this way regularly would probably save a great deal of the taxpayer's money; programs like these are not expensive to organize and the danger of relapse is significantly diminished. It is thus doubly surprising that they have not found their way into most prisons.

A similar lack of interest is discernible on the political stage. The more the danger of nationalism threatens our world, the more frequently we must reckon with the emergence of unpredictable dictators. Dictators are simply a subgroup of people exposed to serious physical and mental jeopardy during childhood. They invest all their innate energies and talents in making sure that they are never placed in that kind of helpless position again. They frequently develop a maniac hatred for one particular group in society (Jews, intellectuals, ethnic groups) who for them represent, vicariously and symbolically, their former persecutors and whom they feel they must overcome if not eradicate at all costs if they want to survive. They expend all their military power on protecting themselves from a danger that has long since ceased to exist except in their imaginations and are all but inaccessible to logical arguments in connection with that danger. Thus in order to achieve any kind of constructive and productive communication with them we would need to know a great deal about the childhood of these people and the dynamics of childhood in general. Unhappily this is normally not the case and it is hard to find anyone who would be prepared to act upon the results of such an inquiry. The tendency is to trust the destructive measures of direct confrontation rather than the productive fruits of direct communication. But it is not enough to know that we are dealing with dangerous individuals who ought to be "taken out of circulation" before they can kill other people, or to know that the ethnic group in question only has a symbolic significance for the dictator. The point is to understand the motives behind his maniac actions on the basis of his life history and not to play his game, not to be maneuvered into the role of persecutor, thus playing along with the role assigned to us in the dictator's own personal reenactment or scenario. Threats and the use of destructive weaponry can set off paradoxical reactions in individuals laboring under a legacy of serious humiliation. They help dictators to cement their hardened positions, to exploit the lack of contacts to cover their tracks even more effectively, and to profit from the image of the persecuted victim.

There are many areas where concern with early childhood can represent a liberation from age-old blind alleys. One of these is school. Here the findings of the neuro-biologists have yet to be given any real credence. Many teachers cannot imagine a school system without punishment and penalization. But we know beyond doubt that punishment has at best a short-term "positive" effect. In the long run, the exertion of force merely serves to reinforce aggressive behavior on the part of children and adolescents. If children from a background of domestic violence have to devote all their attention to averting danger, they will hardly be able to concentrate on the subject matter they are being taught. They may well expend a great deal of effort on observing the teacher so as to be prepared for the physical "correction" that they feel, fatalistically, to be inevitable. In reality as they see it, they can hardly afford to develop an interest in what their teachers are trying to tell them. Yet more blows, yet more punishment are hardly likely to allay this effect; on the other hand, understanding for these children's fears could quite literally "move mountains." But the teacher must never play down the reality of the abused child if he or she really wants to help. And helping instead of punishing would be to the advantage of the teacher and his role as an instructor. But teachers who have themselves grown up with punishment favor punishment in the face of all the logic that militates against it because they have learned at a very early stage to believe in its efficacy. Neither in their own childhood nor during their training as teachers have they had the opportunity to develop a sensibility for the sufferings of children.

We come across the same phenomenon in the field of legislation. As long as we are unaware of the degree to which the right to human dignity has been denied us in our own childhood, it is anything but easy to truly concede that right to our children, however sincerely we may wish to do so. Frequently we believe we are acting in the interests of the children and fail to realize that we may be doing the very opposite, simply because we have learned to be unfeeling in this respect at such an early stage that the effects of this inculcation are stronger than all the things we learn later. We can see this from an actual instance of present-day legislation. Only a short while ago, 1997, the German Parliament expressly conceded natural parents the right to physical correction. This right is only denied to non-blood relatives: teachers, foster-parents, guardians etc. So we see that the majority of the parliamentarians (4/5) are firmly convinced that in certain cases corporal punishment meted out by the parents can have a salutary effect. The argument persistently advanced for this was that physical force should not be prohibited because this phenomenon could be drawn upon to acquaint children with the dangers lying in wait for them on the roads, thus helping them to learn to protect themselves.

But the only thing a beaten child will learn is to fear its parents, not to be careful on the roads. This way, children will also learn to play down their own pain and feel guilty. Being subjected to physical attacks they are defenseless to fend off merely instill in them a "gut" conviction that children obviously merit neither protection nor respect. This false message is then stored in the children's bodies as information and will influence their view of the world and their later attitude to their own children. Such children will be unable to defend their right to human dignity, unable to recognize physical pain as a danger signal and act accordingly. Even their immune system may be affected. In the absence of other persons to model their behavior on, without knowing or at least helping witnesses, these children will see the language of violence and hypocrisy as the only really effective means of communication. Naturally enough, they will avail themselves of that language themselves when they grow up because adults will normally elect to keep suppressed feelings of powerlessness in a state of suppression. Unfortunately, many of us defend the old system of care-giving with all the energy and conviction we can muster. This may be the reason behind this astounding decision to vote against a ban on corporal punishment.

This universal denial of sufferings most of us have been through also leads to a situation where even in cases of mass murder hardly anyone takes any real interest in the origins and causes of such bottomless hatred. All kinds of factors are examined with great care but no one ever asks where and how the perpetrators of such acts acquired these models of violence. We live in a society which regards hatred as innate, that is to say God-given. It is a society that refuses to see that we keep on producing hatred by inculcating models of violence into our children, behavior patterns that can prove stronger than anything they may learn at a later stage. There is a widespread tendency to blame all kinds of uncongenial things on the education system but education to violence begins much earlier and there is nothing that schools can do about those cases where a child has grown up devoid of an empathic home environment, without anyone prepared to relate and sympathize with his or her distress.

Equally surprising is the lack of interest shown by biographers about the initial, all-important imprint left on people by the treatment given them in their early years. With the exception of psychohistorians, hardly any biographer has delved into the childhood of political leaders, individuals whose sometimes fateful decisions can mean life or death, happiness or horror for millions of people. In all the thousands of books about Hitler or Stalin hardly any mention is made of the tell-tale details of their childhood. And where mention is made of them, lack of psychological knowledge leads to their being played down and denied any crucial significance. But there is much to learn from these facts. We can see this more clearly from two contrasting examples: Stalin and Gorbachev.

Stalin was the only child of an alcoholic who beat him soundly every day and a mother who never protected him, was beaten herself and usually stayed away from home. Like Hitler's mother she had already lost three children when her son was born. Joseph, the only surviving child, never knew with any certainty whether his father might not decide to kill him at the next opportunity. When he grew up, his suppressed panic fear was transformed into paranoia, the maniac conviction that everyone else was out to kill him. That was why in the 1930s he had millions of people slaughtered or put into concentration camps. The impression one has is that when all is said and done the all-powerful and idolized dictator was nothing other than a helpless child still fighting a hopeless battle against the overwhelming threat of a brutal father. In the trials orchestrated against thinkers and writers Stalin was perhaps trying to prevent his own father from killing the little boy he once was. Naturally he had no knowledge of this. If he had, it might have saved millions of lives.

A very different picture is presented by the Gorbachev family, where there was no tradition of child-maltreatment but instead a tradition of respect for the child and his needs. The consequences can be observed from the behavior displayed by the adult Gorbachev. He has given ample evidence of qualities hardly any other living statesman has demonstrated to the same degree: the courage to look facts in the face and to seek flexible solutions, respect for others, give-and-take in dialog situations, absence of hypocrisy, a complete absence of grandeur in the conduct of his personal life. He has never been driven by blind self-assertion to make absurd decisions. Both his parents and his grandparents (the latter looked after him during the war years) appear to have been people with an unusual capacity for love and affection. The unanimous verdict on Gorbachev's father, who died in 1976, is that he was a lovable, modest man, amicable and peaceable in his dealings with others, a man who was never heard to raise his voice. The mother is described as sturdy, sincere and cheerful. Even after her son had become a prominent personality, she went on living modestly and happily in her small farmhouse. Gorbachev's childhood also supplies further proof that even severest penury will have no adverse effect on the character of a child as long as that child's personal integrity is not damaged by hypocrisy, cruelty, abuse, corporal punishment, and psychological humiliation. Stalin's regime of terror, the horrors of war, the brutal occupation of his country, immense poverty, crippling physical labor – all these things were part and parcel of Gorbachev's youth. But a child can survive all that unscathed as long as the emotional atmosphere prevailing at home provides protection and security. One incident may serve to illustrates the atmosphere I am referring to. At the end of the war Mikhail Gorbachev was unable to attend school for 3 months because he had no shoes to wear. When his father was told of this (he was wounded and had been committed to a field hospital) he wrote to his wife saying that she must at all costs ensure that Mischa could go back to school because he was such an avid scholar. The mother sold the last of her sheep for 1,500 rubles and bought her son a pair of military boots. His grandfather procured a warm coat for him and at the request of his grandson another one for a friend of his.

Protection and respect for the needs of a child – this is surely something we ought to be able to take for granted. But it is far from being the case. We live in a world peopled by individuals who have grown up deprived of their rights, deprived of respect. As adults they then attempt to regain those rights by force (blackmail, threats, the use of weapons). As Gorbachev's childhood is apparently much more the exception than the rule, the society we live in continues to turn a blind eye to the facts of child abuse in all its forms. Thousands of professors at hundreds of universities teach all manner of subjects, but there is not one single university chair for research into child abuse and cruelty to children. How strange, when we recall that the majority of the people living on this earth are victims of precisely that kind of treatment! It is entirely conceivable that the world as we know it might come to an end as a result of the consequence of those ubiquitous violations of human dignity. At all events, it is high time that we investigated the regularities discernible behind each and every individual case.

As a priority commitment for the next decade, the United Nations Organization has declared its allegiance to the idea and implementation of Education for Peace. This cannot be achieved by fine words alone. We need to set an example to our children as the people who will decide what the next generation will look like, and show them that coexistence and communication without violence is actually possible. There are an ever greater number of parents who are capable of doing so and who are aware of the far-reaching implications of their own behavior. Many of them agree that physical force against children should be banned by law.

This verified and firmly established knowledge cannot but spread, albeit gradually, in the millennium to come, even though at present the number of people who have understood what is at stake is small. But if this group succeeds in getting physical correction banned by law – as has already happened in nine European countries – then the next generation will grow up without spanking and beating, and that means growing up free of a legacy that can only set them off on a course that is fateful indeed. It is realistic to hope that this fact will lead to an increase in the number of knowing witnesses and hence to a swift change in general mentality.

26
Why Do We Hurt Our Children?
by James Kimmel

As a psychologist who specialized in working with emotionally disturbed children, and as a person who has a special fondness for children, it is extremely troublesome to me that punishment, both physical and otherwise, is an intrinsic part of child rearing in the United States. None of my three children, now adults, were ever punished. Just as people who state, "I was spanked and punished and I turned out OK," my children are able to say, "I was never spanked or punished and I turned out OK." And based on the kind of people they are as adults, I would agree that, not only did they turn out OK, but they are much more caring of others, including their children, than most of their contemporaries. They do not, of course, punish their children.

However, I do not wish to prove through my children or my grandchildren that punishment is totally unnecessary in order to grow up to be a socially appropriate and caring person. We already know this from studies of cultures where children are never punished. I hope to show, instead, that punishing children is a malevolent act that is harmful to children and, ultimately, to the community and society in which it takes place. The punishment of one human being by another is behavior in which the punisher has, or believes he has, the right to hurt and violate a person he perceives as his social inferior. Punishing another individual of one's species is a human cultural invention. It is not found in all cultures nor in the animal world. Its utilization as a child-rearing method seems to go hand in hand with the development of civilization.

A person hurting another as a result of a temporary loss of emotional control is not punishment. Such behavior is a different form of violence. Punishment is a deliberate, controlled act with a conscious purpose. It is, of course, a terrible, troublesome, and dangerous fact that, in our society, parental loss of control, accompanied by physical and verbal abuse of children, is tolerated. However, such behavior is not the subject of this paper. Our society, although it may not do much to prevent it, does not openly condone child abuse. But it does openly condone and sanction punishing children, physically and otherwise. What bothers me so much about punishing children is that it is a conscious effort to hurt them physically and/or emotionally. I find it hard to understand, even when it is explained as a way of teaching them proper behavior, why someone would intentionally choose to hurt the life they contributed to creating (or chose to care for through adoption.) I also find it incredible that parents, and many authorities in the areas of mental and physical health, child development, and human morality, cannot see that by hurting children, we are teaching them that it is moral and right to hurt other human beings.

The Origins Of Punishment

It is likely that punishment initially developed in our species as a method to control and direct the behavior of animals by hurting them. It later was applied by humans to other humans to control individual behavior and thinking. The fact that punishment can modify behavior is well-founded.

Research studies on rats, as well as other animals, have clearly indicated that by inflicting pain on them, we can control to a great extent what they do or don't do (Bermant)*, a fact known by farmers and animal trainers for thousands of years. Human thinking can also be altered by punishment and has been utilized throughout civilization by monarchs, dictators, slave owners, authoritarian states, and religious institutions to control deviant and non-conforming individuals.

We do not know when punishment first became a method used to direct children's development. I have never read about a hunter-gatherer society that punishes their children as part of child care. In ancient civilizations, and throughout the history of civilization, punishing children was a common practice (deMause), and the practice continues today in much of the civilized world. Punishment is and has been a commonly accepted part of American child-rearing (deMause, Beekman). It is perceived as a legitimate and appropriate form of discipline. Its legitimacy in human relationships has few parallels in American life, especially since the abolition of slavery. Other than children, only convicted criminals are legally allowed to be punished. But children do not even have the rights of criminals, as they are allowed to be punished without a trial. The closest parallel to punishing children would be the punitive ways in which we domesticate and train young animals so that they will serve, submit to, and entertain us. When we punish our children, we serve to perpetuate the Western civilization belief that children are, like animals, inferior beings who need to be tamed, trained, and controlled.

Punishment and Distrust

Obviously, the decision, felt necessity, or compulsion to punish another person reflects a lack of trust in that person, whether it be in the relationship of governments to citizens, tyrants to subjects, slave owners to slaves, wardens to prisoners, teachers to students, or parents to children. The

---

*For references, see: http://goo.gl/voV7U

advocates of punishing children (which include some past and present "experts" on child development) have a condescending and ugly view of children which is embedded in an even uglier view of the human species. Humans are not, in their eyes, a naturally caring and social species, but a species in which the individual is born anti-social and governed solely by self concern and self-interest. They further believe that children resist socialization, so it must be imposed on them by adults.

There is no recognition, in this perception of the human individual as selfish, alienated, and basically separate from all others, to the fact that sociability, socialization, and the ability to trust develop naturally through appropriate nurturing in childhood. The quality of basic trust, as originally formulated by the psychologist Eric Erikson, is the foundation for a healthy personality (Evans). Its meaning to Erikson and his followers was that during the first year of life, a baby learns that those who care for him can be trusted to satisfy his basic needs. From this secure base the infant learns to trust himself and the world. I prefer to describe basic trust as the experience of a baby or young child that there is a person there for him, who affirms his life and well-being by providing the nurturing relationship that he genetically and biologically evolved to have after birth. Without such an experience during the first stage of life, an infant does not develop the full trust in others that is essential for healthy human emotional and social development.

The need for an infant to develop basic trust in those who care for him has become widely accepted by virtually all health-care specialists. It is not always expressed in such terms, nor is it always achieved, but we all seem to know that babies and children need "love". Much less emphasis has been given to the need for parents to develop basic trust in their children. They may love them, but do they trust them? In fact, many American authorities on infant and child care have sent the message that children, including infants, cannot be trusted. Babies and young children are frequently portrayed as being manipulative and wanting to make their parents' life miserable, as if their need and desire to be with their parents, and to be nurtured by them, is not genuine (Spock, Turtle).

I do not believe that genuine trust can develop in a relationship unless both parties have trust in each other. *In the parent-child relationship, the child learns to trust his parents when his need for nurturing is regularly met.* But this development of trust can only occur if the parent's response to the child is based on the belief that the child's expression of his need for nurturing is genuine, that the child is not just trying to "get his own way"; and is not out to make the parent's life difficult. Misery, unhappiness, and a struggle for power often do become a part of the parent-child interaction, especially in a society such as our own which does not trust and does not validate the nurturing requirements of children. If the relationship of parent and child does become a continual struggle, it is not because the child's motivation is to punish the parent, but because his need for nurturing is not being met. It is also true that a child, as he matures, may begin to behave in ways to punish his parents, but this can only occur if his parents have regularly punished him.

The use of punishment by parents is a clear indication that there has been an insufficient development of trust between parent and child in the early formative years of the child's development. Most American parents punish their children. Most also begin punishing them, and using the threat of punishment, at a very early age (usually in infancy). Children grow up believing that the punishment they received was deserved, and that they were harmful, bad, and not trustworthy. Many, as adults, who lack a foundation of parental trust, do not trust, or even like, themselves. They perceive their needs, especially their need for nurturing, caring, kindness, love, and intimacy, as "bad", selfish, indulgent, harmful, and a burden put on others. Some spend their entire lifetime feeling guilty towards their parents. Often, they begin in adolescence to self-destruct, punishing themselves for burdening their parents, for having been born, for being alive.

The Most Common Methods Of Punishing Children

Corporal punishment in the form of spanking (even in infancy) is the most common way children are punished in America. Slapping, hitting and beating with the hand or straps and other instruments closely follow. *NBC News* has reported that about 90 percent of U.S. parents spank their children. In addition, a 1992 survey reported that 59 percent of pediatricians support the practice ("When Spankings Are Abuse"). It is important to recognize that in our society most parents and many of our infant and child care authorities, do not classify spanking as hitting or physical punishment. By a magnificent denial of reality, it is often described as a "love tap" or "pat" or "harmless swat" or "loving reminder". Since spanking has traditionally been administered in the United States to almost all children for generations, it is considered a natural part of growing up, the same as feeding.

Other more bizarre methods of corporal punishment, such as burning children with fire and other forms of heat, having them kneel on hard objects, or forcing them to stand for many hours, are less common than they once were, but they are still practiced today. We do not know the current extent of their use, nor do we know the current extent of other kinds of physical torture. Throughout civilization, until fairly recently, there have been various kinds of commercial items produced to punish children; including whips, the notorious cat of nine tails, cages, and various shackling devices (Beekman). Since these products are no longer openly advertised and sold, one would expect, or at least hope, that they are not used any more to punish children.

While many countries now outlaw the physical punishment of children, only Austria and the Scandinavian countries completely ban hitting them. However, in the United States, corporal punishment of children by parents is legal and widely practiced. It is also legal in the educational system, despite the fact that it is prohibited in the schools of almost all other industrialized nations. The US, Canada and one state in Australia still continue the practice. Thirty-one of the states in the U.S. have banned corporal punishment in their schools. The twenty three others continue to allow teachers to hit and paddle their students when they deem it necessary (Corporal Punishment Fact Sheet). As a nation, we have been slow to understand the harmful effects that hitting has on our children, and we continue to defend our right to continue to hit them. We do not seem to be concerned that spanking and physically punishing our children creates a new generation who will in turn, continue to physically hurt their children. Based on our belief in the value of corporal punishment we are, in fact, likely to encourage our children to use it on our grandchildren.

It is frightening that many parents, educators, and others who are involved in child care today act out on children the cruel physical imposition that was inflicted on them by their parents and other care-givers while they were growing up. But even more frightening to me than the passage of physical cruelty to children through generations, is the passage of the belief that punishing children is a necessary part of raising them. Even parents and child-care experts who do not believe in corporal punishment advocate other kinds of punishment such as "time-out" and "logical consequences". (Salk, "When Spankings Are Abuse"). Although many of these methods, which are designed to get children to behave, are viewed as appropriate ways to discipline children, they are, in reality, punishments, the purpose of which is to get children to obey their parents' rules and regulations by imposing on them parental power and authority. The following are some of the ways, other than physical punishment, that are frequently used by parents to punish their children. These were not originally or specifically created as tools to help parents to get their children to behave properly. In general, these methods have been borrowed from the traditional methods used to punish adults who had committed crimes or violated laws, rules, customs, or conventional ways of behaving.

Isolation and Confinement

Isolation and confinement usually go together. A child is sent to his room, or made to stand or sit in a corner and usually not permitted to be with, or relate to others. The currently popular "time-out" is, of course, confinement, and also isolation, if the child must be alone during the "time-out" period. Less openly discussed forms of this type of punishment are the practices of tying up or chaining children, locking them in rooms, closets, cars, sheds or other areas of confinement. In general, isolation and confinement are for a brief time. However, it is not uncommon for the time period to extend into hours, and although much less common, can extend sometimes to days, weeks, and even months. Basically, isolation and confinement give children the message that they are inferior and unfit to be with other humans. Many children, if they are frequently punished in this manner will come to believe that they are different, "crazy" and unfit when compared to other children who do not seem to require or receive this type of banishment from society. Often, as they mature, these children act in accordance with what they have been made to believe about themselves.

Deprivation

Another method by which we attempt to teach children to behave is to deprive them of things. Most children are no longer sent to bed without supper. They are, however, denied privileges. Frequent items that are denied include dessert, sweets, toys, allowance or spending money, TV, music, movies, the car, the telephone, friends, or whatever the child likes and is important to him. The length of time of the specific deprivation varies greatly, depending upon, among other things, the particular family, the nature of the misbehavior, and the age of the child. But all forms of deprivation – regardless of their length – teach children that their parents have the power to make their lives miserable by taking away what has meaning to them. Who would trust, or even like, someone with such power?

Grounding

Grounding is similar to and overlaps the punishments of deprivation and confinement, but it is much worse. Here the focus is more on prohibiting activity away from the home, rather than on denying that which is external and material. It is being confined to the house rather than confined to a room in the house. The child is not allowed to go and to do. He is "grounded", like a plane or "docked," like a ship, made to be immobile, temporarily "out of commission". He has lost, for a time, his freedom to move about, his freedom to be fully alive and to grow. The punishment of grounding is, ironically, a major way to teach children to be defiant and disobedient towards their parents, because it usually attacks life and growth in relation to one's peers. One can tolerate, for a time, starvation and imprisonment. It is more difficult to lose one's freedom to act and to be, especially for children.

Withdrawal of Affection

Highly recommended, as a means to control children's behavior, even by supposed liberal and progressive child care experts (Spock, Salk), is the punishment known as withdrawal of affection. Why it is necessary for a parent to consciously do this, is puzzling to me because withdrawal of affection seems to occur automatically (at least temporarily), to most people when someone (including one's child) does something we strongly dislike or which hurts us. Momentary loss of affectionate or tender feelings toward another is a natural part of human relationships and serves to communicate to a significant other what we, as an individual, personally like or dislike. Humans are able to enhance this automatic non-verbal communication with language. However, even without language, the message gets across. Babies communicate their likes and dislikes quite effectively, without a fully-developed language, all the time – that is, if they have someone who is attentively listening and watching.

The communication of both positive and negative feelings is an important way that our species learns to live with, accommodate to, and collaborate with one another. It is an essential part of the human nurturing process. Mother and child are continually accommodating to each other: finding mutually comfortable nursing and carrying positions, dealing with biting of the breast as the child grows teeth, accommodation to the child's increasing development and changing capabilities, the birth of a sibling, and, from the moment of birth, the parents' cultural values and priorities.

Affectionate feelings, and the absence of such feelings, are spontaneous reactions in human relationships. When affection is consciously withdrawn as a means to control another, we are dealing with a different kind of human interaction than the integrative one described in the previous paragraph. Exploiting another person's emotional vulnerability is not an integrative act but rather an act which ultimately alienates the other person. It is a dishonest use of love. It is fake love. The conscious withdrawal of affection by a parent in order to get the child to behave in the manner the parent desires is simply a way of exploiting the child's need for affection from the parent. *It is treating caring and love as commodities which can be given or taken away whenever the parent wishes.* Affection becomes a power tool, a bribe, rather than an emotion. When withdrawal of affection and love is consciously and regularly used as a way to punish children, their human capacity to love, cherish, and trust another person, becomes tarnished. The child's critical need for parental love, security, and protection has been abused.

Some Other Ways Frequently Used To Punish Children

There are, of course, other ways that children have been, and continue to be, punished than the ones I have already detailed. We no longer punish adults by public whipping or by exposing them to public scorn by placing them in a pillory or stock or ducking stool. But children are still punished, if not by such extreme measures, then by intentionally embarrassing and humiliating them. It is considered proper in rearing children to make them feel ashamed about their behavior, and to humiliate and disgrace them in front of others. Dunce caps, as well as wearing and carrying signs about one's bad behavior, are still used by parents, teachers and school officials, although not as much as they were in the early part of this century. Ridicule and verbal abuse, both in the home and in public, are common methods used by parents and other authoritarians to make children feel badly about themselves and their behavior.

Another common way of punishing children is to frighten them. They are told about, and threatened with, images of bogeymen, monsters, God, the devil, animals, hell, or whatever humans can invent, to terrorize children in order to get them to behave. This form of mental torture is preferred by many parents because it allows the parent to let someone else do the "dirty work". It is not the parent who will harm the child but somebody, or something, else. This form of punishment makes children a little "crazy", and when used extensively, very "crazy".

One other commonly used punishment, which on the surface appears to be benign, is the assignment of chores or additional chores as punishment for "bad" behavior. Of course, this kind of punishment is not so benign if the chores are extremely strenuous or so prolonged that they can be physically harmful to the child. In addition, if the chores hinder the child greatly from other more desirable activities, the child is then receiving "double" punishment, which is not only unfair, but doubly painful. The assignment of chores as punishment can lead children to resent and hate the chores that need to be accepted as a natural part of learning, working, and caring for oneself and others. Chore-punishment may not hurt a child as much as other punishments, but, as do all punishments, it teaches children that it is all right to impose your will on another if you believe your cause is just.

Punishment And Parent-Child Alienation

It is strange to me that parents who punish their child do not seem to recognize that, not only are they harming the child, but they are also harming their relationship with the child. But perhaps they do recognize this fact, and that is why the statement by parents, "This hurts me more than it does you," has long been a part of the child punishment ritual. Intentionally hurting another person leads the injured person to be afraid of, and distrustful of, the person who has hurt them, especially if the hurting person indicates that they have the right to hurt the victim, and that they will continue to hurt the victim, whenever they deem it necessary.

Punishment of children alienates them from their parents and increases children's distrust of those who, biologically, are supposed to provide them with the security of feeling and knowing that they are not separate in the world. Children, because they are dependent on their parents for so many essential things, usually have little choice but to accept the reality that punishment and hurt are part of their relationship with their parents. However, as they get older, children of punitive parents are more likely, as compared with children who are not punished, to lie to, to not confide in, and to conceal their behaviors from their parents. This is not part of the normal growth pattern of becoming a person who is less dependent on their parents, but rather a reflection of the fact that these children do not trust their parents to be understanding, empathic, or to treat them kindly. The punishment these children received when they were younger has taught them that when they are involved in problematic behavior, their personal integrity and rights as a person will be ignored, violated and not respected by their parents. *They have received the true message of punishment, which is to banish behavior which appears to be negative, rather than to try to understand it.*

Does Punishing Children Work?

Does punishing children work? It definitely helps parents to believe that they are in control of their child. They are able to relax for a while until the next misdeed. Does punishment change children's behavior? Yes, but only for a brief time. Usually children will continue to do the same things they were punished for, if they think they can get away with it.

One of the troubles with punishment as a way to teach children proper social behavior, aside from the infliction of pain, is that it makes children feel weak, impotent and incapable. Punishment teaches children to look to external authority to decide for them how they should behave, rather than looking to themselves. They do not learn how, in collaboration with others, to make choices; they do not learn how to decide what is good for them and for those who are important to them. What they learn instead is to submit to authority and power, to obey. By being punished and treated as inferior beings, they become inferior beings – they do not develop the power of the human individual to love and trust. Children who are regularly punished learn to fear their parents. They learn the behaviors that their parents like and don't like and also, how to hide these behaviors from their parents. *They develop "proper" behavior out of fear, not choice.*

Some children openly defy their punitive parents. These children usually end up getting into worse trouble with their parents, and with other authorities as they mature. Most children, however, go underground. In order to protect themselves from parental power they develop a "good", submissive-to-authority, social pose to hide their secret misbehaviors and improper thoughts and feelings. Their social behavior is not genuine because it has little to do with who they really are. Once out of the realm of authoritarian control, they adopt new ways and new codes consistent with the values and priorities of their peers. They go in any direction the wind blows to avoid disapproval and to gain approval. The lack of respect their parents had for them has prevented them from developing respect for themselves.

Why We Hurt Our Children

The question that must be asked is why we are, and have been, so willing to hurt our children in order to get them to behave – to treat them as criminals, slaves and animals. Of course, we are, in part, following the traditional ways of treating children for centuries of civilization. But there is more to it than just tradition. We have in the past century learned a great deal more than we knew before about children's emotional and social development and their mental health. This information is not kept secret from the public. Most of us even seem to recognize and accept that what happens to children in their early years has a great deal to do with the kind of persons they become. Yet, we continue to punish them. Do we not see the harm we do? Why do we not stop consciously hurting our children?

For some parents, whose own punishment as children was accompanied by rage, hatred, and sadism, punishing their own children is an opportunity for them to legally inflict pain on another human being – a chance to get back at someone for the pain that they suffered. But for most parents, it is a matter of controlling behavior which they were made to control in their own childhood. It is a matter of ignorance, of passing on malevolent and inappropriate behavior toward children which they learned to accept as appropriate in their own childhoods. They are acting from an attitude that says it is just and right to hurt children in order to achieve certain ends. They will defend their belief that their own parents were right to punish them, that they are right to punish their children, and that their children will be right to punish their children. "After all," so many parents say, "how else can you get them to behave?" And many, even when they are told "how", still punish their children. On a deeper psychological and social level, parental punishers of their children do so because their children make them anxious by confronting them with behaviors and feelings which the parents themselves have learned to hide, suppress, repress, and disown. They must condition their children as they were conditioned.

Children threaten our identity, security, and reality. We harm them in order to stop our perceived threat that their behavior will harm us. It is a myth that we punish children for their own good. We punish children so that we will be secure. Our children have the power to elicit our tender and loving feelings. They also have the power to frighten, anger, and embarrass us. From being punished, children learn to distrust and fear their parents. Other than that, children and parents learn nothing. By condoning punishment as a disciplinary tool, we perpetuate the acceptability of the use of force and power to control others. At the same time we perpetuate our ignorance and our fear. We use punishment in order to stop behavior rather than having the courage to confront and understand it. By openly dealing with the underlying causes of the child's behavior, both parent and child have the opportunity to get a better and more realistic view of the child's actions, and any potential danger to the child and/or to the parent. We evolved to protect children from harm, not to harm them.

The belief in our society that punishing children will make them into social beings reveals our alienation from the socialization process that is normal and natural to our species. *We become genuine social beings from developing in relation to tender, nurturing, and non-harmful others.* Alienated from our own need for tenderness, and hardened since birth by life in a non-nurturing society, we teach our children that punishing them is proper parenting that will help them to grow right and to be good. We do not seem to understand that punishment does not make children social, it merely teaches them to fit into a society which separates us from each other – a society which is not based on the human capacity for tenderness or on concern for another, but on the absence of these. Punishing our children sabotages the nurturing and protective feelings that we evolved to have towards them. It destroys the unity of parent and child. It teaches us to violate the rights of others. As a socially condoned practice in child rearing, it damages and insults the human species.

27
On Seeing Children as "Cute"
by John Holt

We should try to get out of the habit of seeing little children as cute. By this I mean that we should try to be more aware of what it is in children to which we respond and to tell which responses are authentic, respectful, and life-enhancing, and which are condescending or sentimental. Our response to a child is authentic when we are responding to qualities in the child that are not only real but valuable human qualities we would be glad to find in someone of any age. It is condescending when we respond to qualities that enable us to feel superior to the child. It is sentimental when we respond to qualities that do not exist in the child but only in some vision or theory that we have about children.

In responding to children as cute, we are responding to many qualities that rightly, as if by healthy instinct, appeal to us. Children tend to be, among other things, healthy, energetic, quick, vital, vivacious, enthusiastic, resourceful, intelligent, intense, passionate, hopeful, trustful, and forgiving – they get very angry but do not, like us, bear grudges for long. Above all, they have a great capacity for delight, joy, and sorrow. But we should not think of these qualities or virtues as "childish," the exclusive property of children. They are *human* qualities. We are wise to value them in people of all ages. When we think of these qualities as childish, belonging only to children, we invalidate them, make them seem as things we should "outgrow" as we grow older. Thus we excuse ourselves for carelessly losing what we should have done our best to keep. Worse yet, we teach the children this lesson; most of the bright and successful ten-year-olds I have known, though they still kept the curiosity of their younger years, had learned to be ashamed of it and hide it. Only "little kids" went around all the time asking silly questions. To be grown-up was to be cool, impassive, unconcerned, untouched, invulnerable. Perhaps women are taught to feel this way less than men; perhaps custom gives them a somewhat greater license to be childlike, which they should take care not to lose.

But though we may respond authentically to many qualities of children, we too often respond either condescendingly or sentimentally to many others – condescendingly to their littleness, weakness, clumsiness, ignorance, inexperience, incompetence, helplessness, dependency, immoderation, and lack of any sense of time or proportion; and sentimentally to made-up notions about their happiness, carefreeness, innocence, purity, nonsexuality, goodness, spirituality, and wisdom. These notions are mostly nonsense. Children are not particularly happy or carefree; they have as many worries and fears as many adults, often the same ones. What makes them seem happy is their energy and curiosity, their involvement with life; they do not waste much time in brooding. Children are the farthest thing in the world from spiritual. They are not abstract, but concrete. They are animals and sensualists; to them, what *feels* good *is* good. They are self-absorbed and selfish. They have very little ability to put themselves in another person's shoes, to imagine how he feels. This often makes them inconsiderate and sometimes cruel, but whether they are kind or cruel, generous or greedy, they are always so on impulse rather than by plan or principle. They are barbarians, primitives, about whom we are also often sentimental. Some of the things (which are not school subjects and can't be "taught") that children don't know, but only learn in time and from living, are things they will be better for knowing. Growing up and growing older are not always or only or necessarily a decline and a defeat. Some of the understanding and wisdom that can come with time is real – which is why children are attracted by the natural authority of any adults who do respond authentically and respectfully to them.

One afternoon I was with several hundred people in an auditorium of a junior college when we heard outside the building the passionate wail of a small child. Almost everyone smiled, chuckled, or laughed. Perhaps there was something legitimately comic in the fact that one child should, without even trying, be able to interrupt the supposedly important thoughts and words of all these adults. But beyond this was something else, the belief that the feelings, pains, and passions of children were not *real*, not to be taken seriously. If we had heard outside the building the voice of an adult crying in pain, anger, or sorrow, we would not have smiled or laughed but would have been frozen in wonder and terror. Most of the time, when it is not an unwanted distraction, or a nuisance, the crying of children strikes us as funny. We think, there they go again, isn't it something the way children cry, they cry about almost anything. But there is nothing funny about children's crying. Until he has learned from adults to exploit his childishness and cuteness, a small child does not cry for trivial reasons but out of need, fear, or pain.

Once, coming into an airport, I saw just ahead of me a girl of about seven or eight. Hurrying up the carpeted ramp, she tripped and fell down. She did not hurt herself but quickly picked herself up and walked on. But looking around on everyone's face I saw indulgent smiles, expressions of "isn't that cute?" They would not have thought it funny or cute if an adult had fallen down but would have worried about his pain and embarrassment.

The trouble with sentimentality, and the reason why it always leads to callousness and cruelty, is that it is abstract and unreal. We look at the lives and concerns and troubles of children as we might look at actors on a stage, a comedy as long as it does not become a nuisance. And so, since their feelings and their pain are neither serious nor real, any pain we may cause them is not real either. In any conflict of interest with us, they must give way; only our needs are real. Thus when an adult wants for his own pleasure to hug and kiss a child for whom his embrace is unpleasant or terrifying, we easily say that the child's unreal feelings don't count, it is only the adult's real needs that count. People who treat children like living dolls when they are feeling good may treat them like unliving dolls when they are feeling bad. "Little angels" quickly become "little devils."

Even in those happy families in which the children are not jealous of each other, not competing for a scarce supply of attention and approval, but are more or less good friends, they don't think of each other as cute and are not sentimental about children littler than they are. Bigger children in happy families may be very tender and careful toward the little ones. But such older children do not tell themselves and would not believe stories about the purity and goodness of the smaller child. They know very well that the young child is littler, clumsier, more ignorant, more in need of help, and much of the time more unreasonable and troublesome. Because children do not think of each other as cute, they often seem to be harder on each other than we think we would be. They are blunt and unsparing. But on the whole this frankness, which accepts the other as a complete person, even if one not always or altogether admired, is less harmful to the children than the way many adults deal with them.

Much of what we respond to in children as cute is not strength or virtue, real or imagined, but weakness, a quality which gives us power over them or helps us to feel superior. Thus we think they are cute partly because they are little. But what is cute about being little? Children understand this very well. They are not at all sentimental about their own littleness. They would rather be big than little, and they want to get big as soon as they can.

How would we feel about children, react to them, deal with them, if they reached their full size in the first two or three years of their lives? We would not be able to go on using them as love objects or slaves or property. We would have no interest in keeping them helpless, dependent, babyish. Since they were grown-up physically, we would want them to grow up in other ways. On their part, they would want to become free, active, independent, and responsible as fast as they could, and since they were full-sized and could not be used any longer as living dolls or super-pets we would do all we could do to help them do so.

Or suppose that people varied in size as much as dogs, with normal adults anywhere from one foot to seven feet tall. We would not then think of the littleness of children as something that was cute. It would simply be a condition, like being bald or hairy, fat or thin. That someone was little would not be a signal for us to experience certain feelings or make important judgments about his character or the kinds of relationships we might have with him.

Another quality of children that makes us think they are cute, makes us smile or get misty-eyed, is their "innocence." What do we mean by this? In part we mean only that they are ignorant and inexperienced. But ignorance is not a blessing, it is a misfortune. Children are no more sentimental about their ignorance than they are about their size. They want to escape their ignorance, to know what's going on, and we should be glad to help them escape it if they ask us and if we can. But by the innocence of children we mean something more – their hopefulness, trustfulness, confidence, their feeling that the world is open to them, that life has many possibilities, that what they don't know they can find out, what they can't do they can learn to do. These are qualities valuable in everyone. When we call them "innocence" and ascribe them only to children, as if they were too dumb to know any better, we are only trying to excuse our own hopelessness and despair.

Today in the Boston Public Garden I watched, as I often do, some infants who were just learning to walk. I used to think their clumsiness, their uncertain balance and wandering course, were cute. Now I tried to watch in a different spirit. For there is nothing cute about clumsiness, any more than littleness. Any adult who found it as hard to walk as a small child, and who did it so badly, would be called severely handicapped. We certainly would not smile, chuckle, and laugh at his efforts – and congratulate ourselves for doing so. Watching the children, I thought of this. And I reminded myself, as I often do when I see a very small child intent and absorbed in what he is doing and I am tempted to think of him as cute, "That child isn't trying to be cute; he doesn't see himself as cute; and he doesn't want to be seen as cute. He is as serious about what he is doing now as any human being can be, and he wants to be taken seriously."

But there is something very appealing and exciting about watching children just learning to walk. They do it so badly, it is so clearly difficult, and in the child's terms may even be dangerous. We know it won't hurt him to fall down, but he can't be sure of that and in any case doesn't like it. Most adults, even many older children, would instantly stop trying to do anything that they did as badly as a new walker does his walking. But the infant keeps on. He is so determined, he is working so hard, and he is so excited; his learning to walk is not just an effort and struggle but a joyous adventure. As I watch this adventure, no less a miracle because we all did it, I try to respond to the child's determination, courage, and pleasure, not his littleness, feebleness, and incompetence. To whatever voice in me says, "Oh, wouldn't it be nice to pick up that dear little child and give him a big hug and kiss," I reply, "No, no, no, that child doesn't want to be picked up, hugged, and kissed, he wants to walk. He doesn't know or care whether I like it or not, he is not walking for the approval or happiness of me or even for his parents beside him, but for himself. It is his show. Don't try to turn him into an actor in your show. Leave him alone to get on with his work."

We often think children are most cute when they are most intent and serious about what they are doing. In our minds we say to the child, "You think that what you are doing is important; we know it's not; like everything else in your life that you take seriously, it is trivial." We smile tenderly at the child carefully patting his mud pie. We feel that mud pie is not serious and all the work he is putting into it is a waste (though we may tell him in a honey-dearie voice that it is a *beautiful* mud pie). But he doesn't know that; in his ignorance he is just as serious as if he were doing something important. How satisfying for us to feel we know better.

We tend to think that children are most cute when they are openly displaying their ignorance and incompetence. We value their dependency and helplessness. They are help objects as well as love objects. Children acting really competently and intelligently do not usually strike us as cute. They are as likely to puzzle and threaten us. We don't like to see a child acting in a way that makes it impossible for us to look down on him or to suppose that he depends on our help. This is of course very true in school. The child whose teachers know that he knows things they don't know may be in trouble. We know, too, how much schools and first-grade teachers hate to have children come to school already knowing how to read. How then will the school teach him? When we see a young child doing anything very well, we are likely to think there is something wrong with him. He is too precocious, he is peculiar, he is going to have troubles someday, he is "acting like an adult," he has "lost his childhood." Many people reacted so to the extraordinarily capable child pupils of the Japanese violin teacher Suzuki. And I remember the sociologist Omar K. Moore telling me that when he first showed that many three-year-olds, given certain kinds of typewriters and equipment to use and experiment with, could very quickly teach themselves to read (which they weren't supposed to have the visual acuity, coordination, or mental ability to do), he received a flood of indignant and angry letters accusing him of mistreating the children.

Children do not like being incompetent any more than they like being ignorant. They want to learn how to do, and do well, the things they see being done by the bigger people around them.

28

10 Ways We Misunderstand Children

by Jan Hunt

1. We expect children to be able to do things before they are ready. We ask an infant to keep quiet. We ask a 2-year-old to sit still. We ask a 4-year-old to clean his room. In all of these situations, we are being unrealistic. We are setting ourselves up for disappointment and setting up the child for repeated failures to please us. Yet many parents ask their young children to do things that even an older child would find difficult. In short, we ask children to stop acting their age.

2. We become angry when a child fails to meet our needs. A child can only do what he can do. If a child cannot do something we ask, it is unfair and unrealistic to expect or demand more, and anger only makes things worse. A 2-year-old can only act like a 2-year-old, a 5-year-old cannot act like a 10-year-old, and a 10-year-old cannot act like an adult. To expect more is unrealistic and unhelpful. There are limits to what a child can manage, and if we don't accept those limits, it can only result in frustration on both sides.

3. We mistrust the child's motives. If a child cannot meet our needs, we assume that he is being defiant, instead of looking closely at the situation from the child's point of view, so we can determine the truth of the matter. In reality, a "defiant" child may be ill, tired, hungry, in pain, responding to an emotional or physical hurt, or struggling with a hidden cause such as a food allergy. Yet we seem to overlook these possibilities in favor of thinking the worst about the child's "personality".

4. We don't allow children to be children. We somehow forget what it was like to be a child ourselves, and expect the child to act like an adult instead of acting his age. A healthy child will be rambunctious, noisy, emotionally expressive, and will have a short attention span. All of these "problems" are not problems at all, but are in fact normal qualities of a normal child. Rather, it is our society and our society's expectations of perfect behavior that are abnormal.

5. We get it backwards. We expect, and demand, that the child meet our needs – for quiet, for uninterrupted sleep, for obedience to our wishes, and so on. Instead of accepting our parental role to meet the child's needs, we expect the child to care for ours. We can become so focused on our own unmet needs and frustrations that we forget that this is a child, who has needs of his own.

6. We blame and criticize when a child makes a mistake. Children have had very little experience in life, and they will inevitably make mistakes. Mistakes are a natural part of learning at any age. Instead of understanding and helping the child, we blame him, as though he should be able to learn everything perfectly the first time. To err is human; to err in childhood is human and unavoidable. Yet we react to each mistake, infraction of a rule, or misbehavior with surprise and disappointment. It makes no sense to understand that a child *will* make mistakes, and then to react as though we think the child should behave perfectly at all times.

7. We forget how deeply blame and criticism can hurt a child. Many parents are coming to understand that physically hurting a child is wrong and harmful, yet many of us forget how painful angry words, insults, and blame can be to a child who can only believe that he is at fault.

8. We forget how healing loving actions can be. We fall into vicious cycles of blame and misbehavior, instead of stopping to give the child love, reassurance, self-esteem, and security with hugs and kind words.

9. We forget that our behavior provides the most potent lessons to the child. It is truly "not what we say but what we do" that the child takes to heart. A parent who hits a child for hitting, telling him that hitting is wrong, is in fact teaching that hitting is right, at least for those in power. It is the parent who responds to problems with peaceful solutions who is teaching his child how to be a peaceful adult. So-called problems present our best opportunity for teaching values, because children learn best when they are learning about real things in real life.

10. We see only the outward behavior, not the love and good intentions inside the child. When a child's behavior disappoints us, we should, more than anything else we do, "assume the best". We should always assume that the child means well and is behaving as well as possible considering all the circumstances (whether obvious or unknown to us), together with his level of experience in life. If we always assume the best about our child, the child will be free to *do* his best. If we give only love, love is all we will receive.

29
Raising Children
Compassionately
by Marshall B. Rosenberg

I've been teaching Nonviolent Communication^{SM} to parents for 30 years. I would like to share some of the things that have been helpful to both myself and to the parents that I've worked with, and to share with you some insights I've had into the wonderful and challenging occupation of parenting.

I'd first like to call your attention to the danger of the word "child", if we allow it to apply a different quality of respect than we would give to someone who is not labeled a child. Let me show you what I am referring to.

In parent workshops that I've done over the years, I've often started by dividing the group into two. I put one group in one room, and the other in a different room, and I give each group the task of writing down on a large paper a dialogue between themselves and another person in a conflict situation. I tell both groups what the conflict is. The only difference is that I tell one group the other person is their child, and to the second group I say the other person is their neighbor.

Then we get back into a large group and we look at these different sheets of paper outlining the dialogue that the groups would have, in the one case thinking that the other person was their child, and in the other case, the neighbor. (And incidentally, I haven't allowed the groups to discuss with the other group who the person was in their situation, so that both groups think that the situation is the same.)

After they've had a chance to scan the written dialogues of both groups, I ask them if they can see a difference in terms of the degree of respect and compassion that was demonstrated. Every time I've done this, the group that was working on the situation with the other person being a child was seen as being less respectful and compassionate in their communication than the group that saw the other person as a neighbor. This painfully reveals to the people in these groups how easy it is to dehumanize someone by the simple process of simply thinking of him or her as "our child."

I had an experience one day that really heightened my awareness of the danger of thinking of people as children. This experience followed a weekend in which I had worked with two groups: a street gang and a police department. I was mediating between the two groups. There had been considerable violence between them, and they had asked that I serve in the role of a mediator. After spending as much time as I did with them, dealing with the violence they had toward each other, I was exhausted. And as I was driving home afterwards, I told myself, I never want to be in the middle of another conflict for the rest of my life.

And of course, when I walked in my back door, my three children were fighting. I expressed my pain to them in a way that we advocate in Nonviolent Communication. I expressed how I was feeling, what my needs were, and what my requests were. I did it this way. I shouted, "When I hear all of this going on right now, I feel extremely tense! I have a real need for some peace and quiet after the weekend I've been through! So would you all be willing to give me that time and space?"

My oldest son looked at me and said, "Would you like to talk about it?" Now, at that moment, I dehumanized him in my thinking. Why? Because I said to myself, "How cute. Here's a nine year old boy trying to help his father." But take a closer look at how I was disregarding his offer because of his age, because I had him labeled as a child. Fortunately I saw that was going on in my head, and maybe I was able to see it more clearly because the work I had been doing between the street gang and the police showed me the danger of thinking of people in terms of labels instead of their humanness.

So instead of seeing him as a child and thinking to myself, "how cute", I saw a human being who was reaching out to another human being in pain, and I said out loud, "Yes, I would like to talk about it". And the three of them followed me into another room and listened while I opened up my heart to how painful it was to see that people could come to a point of wanting to hurt one another simply because they hadn't been trained to see the other person's humanness. After talking about it for 45 minutes I felt wonderful, and as I recall we turned the stereo on and danced like fools for awhile.

So I'm not suggesting that we don't use words like "child" as a short-hand way of letting people know that we're talking about people of a certain age. I'm talking about when we allow labels like this to keep us from seeing the other person as a human being, in a way which leads us to dehumanize the other person because of the things our culture teaches us about "children." Let me show you an extension of what I'm talking about, how the label child can lead us to behave in a way that's quite unfortunate.

Having been educated, as I was, to think about parenting, I thought that it was the job of a parent to make children behave. You see, once you define yourself as an authority, a teacher or parent, in the culture that I was educated in, you then see it as your responsibility to make people that you label a "child" or a "student" behave in a certain way.

I now see what a self-defeating objective this is, because I have learned that any time it's our objective to get another person to behave in a certain way, people are likely to resist no matter what it is we're asking for. This seems to be true whether the other person is 2 or 92 years of age.

This objective of getting what we want from other people, or getting them to do what we want them to do, threatens the autonomy of people, their right to choose what they want to do. And whenever people feel that they're not free to choose what they want to do, they are likely to resist, even if they see the purpose in what we are asking and would ordinarily want to do it. So strong is our need to protect our autonomy, that if we see that someone has this single-mindedness of purpose, if they are acting like they think that they know what's best for us and are not leaving it to us to make the choice of how we behave, it stimulates our resistance.

I'll be forever grateful to my children for educating me about the limitations of the objective of getting other people to do what you want. They taught me that, first of all, I couldn't make them do what I want. I couldn't make them do anything. I couldn't make them put a toy back in the toy box. I couldn't make them make their bed. I couldn't make them eat. Now, that was quite a humbling lesson for me as a parent, to learn about my powerlessness, because somewhere I had gotten it into my mind that it was the job of a parent to make a child behave. And here were these young children teaching me this humbling lesson, that I couldn't make them do anything. All I could do is make them wish they had.

And whenever I would be foolish enough to do that, that is, to make them wish they had, they taught me a second lesson about parenting and power that has proven very valuable to me over the years. And that lesson was that anytime I would make them wish they had, they would make me wish I hadn't made them wish they had. Violence begets violence.

They taught me that any use of coercion on my part would invariably create resistance on their part, which could lead to an adversarial quality in the connection between us. I don't want to have that quality of connection with any human being, but especially not with my children, those human beings that I'm closest to and taking responsibility for. So my children are the last people that I want to get into these coercive games of which punishment is a part.

Now this concept of punishment is strongly advocated by most parents. Studies indicate that about 80% of American parents firmly believe in corporal punishment of children. This is about the same percentage of the population who believes in capital punishment of criminals. So with such a high percentage of the population believing that punishment is justified and necessary in the education of children, I've had plenty of opportunity over the years to discuss this issue with parents, and I'm pleased with how people can be helped to see the limitations of any kind of punishment, if they'll simply ask themselves two questions.

Question number one: What do you want the child to do differently? If we ask only that question, it can certainly seem that punishment sometimes works, because certainly through the threat of punishment or application of punishment, we can at times influence a child to do what we would like the child to do.

However, when we add a second question, it has been my experience that parents see that punishment never works. The second question is: What do we want the child's reasons to be for acting as we would like them to act? It's that question that helps us to see that punishment not only doesn't work, but it gets in the way of our children doing things for reasons that we would like them to do them.

Since punishment is so frequently used and justified, parents can only imagine that the opposite of punishment is a kind of permissiveness in which we do nothing when children behave in ways that are not in harmony with our values. So therefore parents can think only, "If I don't punish, then I give up my own values and just allow the child to do whatever he or she wants". As I'll be discussing below, there are other approaches besides permissiveness, that is, just letting people do whatever they want to do, or coercive tactics such as punishment. And while I'm at it, I'd like to suggest that reward is just as coercive as punishment. In both cases we are using power over people, controlling the environment in a way that tries to force people to behave in ways that we like. In that respect reward comes out of the same mode of thinking as punishment.

There is another approach besides doing nothing or using coercive tactics. It requires an awareness of the subtle but important difference between our objective being to get people to do what we want, which I'm not advocating, and instead being clear that our objective is to create the quality of connection necessary for everyone's needs to get met.

It has been my experience, whether we are communicating with children or adults, that when we see the difference between these two objectives, and we are consciously not trying to get a person to do what we want, but trying to create a quality of mutual concern, a quality of mutual respect, a quality where both parties think that their needs matter and they are conscious that their needs and the other person's well-being are interdependent – it is amazing how conflicts which otherwise seem unresolvable, are easily resolved.

Now, this kind of communication that is involved in creating the quality of connection necessary for everybody's needs to get met is quite different from that communication used if we are using coercive forms of resolving differences with children. It requires a shift away from evaluating children in moralistic terms such as right/wrong, good/bad, to a language based on needs. We need to be able to tell children whether what they're doing is in harmony with our needs, or in conflict with our needs, but to do it in a way that doesn't stimulate guilt or shame on the child's part. So it might require our saying to the child, "I'm scared when I see you hitting your brother, because I have a need for people in the family to be safe," instead of, "It's wrong to hit your brother." Or it might require a shift away from saying, "You are lazy for not cleaning up your room," to saying, "I feel frustrated when I see that the bed isn't made, because I have a real need for support in keeping order in the house."

This shift in language away from classifying children's behavior in terms of right and wrong, and good and bad, to a language based on needs, is not easy for those of us who were educated by teachers and parents to think in moralistic judgments. It also requires an ability to be present to our children, and listen to them with empathy when they are in distress. This is not easy when we have been trained as parents to want to jump in and give advice, or to try to fix things.

So when I'm working with parents, we look at situations that are likely to arise where a child might say something like, "Nobody likes me". When a child says something like that, I believe the child is needing an empathic kind of connection. And by that I mean a respectful understanding where the child feels that we are there and really hear what he or she is feeling and needing. Sometimes we can do this silently, just showing in our eyes that we are with their feelings of sadness, and their need for a different quality of connection with their friends. Or it could involve our saying out loud something like, "So it sounds like you're really feeling sad, because you aren't having very much fun with your friends."

But many parents, defining their role as requiring them to make their children happy all the time, jump in when a child says something like that, and say things like, "Well, have you looked at what you've been doing that might have been driving your friends away?" Or they disagree with the child, saying, "Well, that's not true. You've had friends in the past. I'm sure you'll get more friends." Or they give advice: "Maybe if you'd talk differently to your friends, your friends would like you more."

What they don't realize is that all human beings, when they're in pain, need presence and empathy. They may want advice, but they want that after they've received the empathic connection. My own children have taught me the hard way that, "Dad, please withhold all advice unless you receive a request in writing from us signed by a notary."

Many people believe that it's more humane to use reward than punishment. But both of them I see as power over others, and Nonviolent Communication is based on power with people. And in power with people, we try to have influence not by how we can make people suffer if they don't do what we want, or how we can reward them if they do. It's a power based on mutual trust and respect, which makes people open to hearing each other and learning from each other, and to giving to one another willingly out of a desire to contribute to one another's well-being, rather than out of a fear of punishment or hope for a reward.

We get this kind of power, power with people, by being able to openly communicate our feelings and needs without in any way criticizing the other person. We do that by offering them what we would like from them in a way that is not heard as demanding or threatening. And as I have said, it also requires really hearing what other people are trying to communicate, showing an accurate understanding rather than quickly jumping in and giving advice, or trying to fix things.

For many parents, the way I'm talking about communicating is so different that they say, "Well, it just doesn't seem natural to communicate that way." At just the right time, I read something that Gandhi had written in which he said, "Don't mix up that which is habitual with that which is natural." Gandhi said that very often we've been trained to communicate and act in ways that are quite unnatural, but they are habitual in the sense that we have been trained for various reasons to do it that way in our culture. And that certainly rang true to me in the way that I was trained to communicate with children. The way I was trained to communicate by judging rightness and wrongness, goodness and badness, and the use of punishment was widely used and very easily became habitual for me as a parent. But I wouldn't say that because something is habitual that it is natural.

I learned that it is much more natural for people to connect in a loving, respectful way, and to do things out of joy for each other, rather than using punishment and reward or blame and guilt as means of coercion. But such a transformation does require a good deal of consciousness and effort.

I can recall one time when I was transforming myself from a habitually judgmental way of communicating with my children to the way that I am now advocating. On the day I'm thinking of, my oldest son and I were having a conflict, and it was taking me quite awhile to communicate it in the way that I was choosing to, rather than the way that had become habitual. Almost everything that came into my mind originally was some coercive statement in the form of a judgment of him for saying what he did. So I had to stop and take a deep breath, and think of how to get more in touch with my needs, and how to get more in touch with his needs. And this was taking me awhile. And he was getting frustrated because he had a friend waiting for him outside, and he said, "Daddy, it's taking you so long to talk." And I said, "Let me tell you what I can say quickly: Do it my way or I'll kick your butt". He said, "Take your time, Dad. Take your time".

So yes, I would rather take my time and come from an energy that I choose in communicating with my children, rather than habitually responding in a way that I have been trained to do, when it's not really in harmony with my own values. Sadly, we will often get much more reinforcement from those around us for behaving in a punitive, judgmental way, than in a way that is respectful to our children.

I can recall one Thanksgiving dinner when I was doing my best to communicate with my youngest son in the way that I am advocating, and it was not easy, because he was testing me to the limits. But I was taking my time, taking deep breaths, trying to understand what his needs were, trying to understand my own needs so I could express them in a respectful way. Another member of the family, observing my conversation with my son, but who had been trained in a different way of communicating, reached over at one point and whispered in my ear, "If that was my child, he'd be sorry for what he was saying".

I've talked to a lot of other parents who have had similar experiences who, when they are trying to relate in more human ways with their own children, instead of getting support, often get criticized. People can often mistake what I'm talking about as permissiveness or not giving children the direction they need, instead of understanding that it's a different quality of direction. It's a direction that comes from two parties trusting each other, rather than one party forcing his or her authority on another.

One of the most unfortunate results of making our objective to get our children to do what we want, rather than having our objective be for all of us to get what we want, is that eventually our children will be hearing a demand in whatever we are asking. And whenever people hear a demand, it's hard for them to keep focus on the value of whatever is being requested, because, as I said earlier, it threatens their autonomy, and that's a strong need that all people have. They want to be able to do something when they choose to do it, and not because they are forced to do it. As soon as a person hears a demand, it's going to make any resolution that will get everybody's needs met much harder to come by.

30
Born to Explore
by Missy Willis

"The first and simplest emotion which we discover in the human mind is curiosity." – Edmund Burke

Children are curious creatures. Think about a baby, in your arms, unable to crawl. He reaches for dangling or sparkling earrings, for your glasses, trying to pull them off your face, he tugs on your nose or pokes your eyes or sticks his fingers into your mouth. He leans and reaches and grabs at your food. His eyes follow the movement of people or pets or objects.

Think about crawling babies. They can find the tiniest speck of dirt in your newly vacuumed carpet. They find dead bugs on the floor that you swear were never there. They chew on shoes, toys, and yes, even electrical cords. They spin the toilet paper off the roll, splash in the toilet water and pull books off shelves and containers out of cabinets. They have no concept of mine or yours. Everything that is within their reach is theirs to explore; the visitor's purse, your guest's meal, a grocery bag.

Think about young children. They touch everything. They want to pick up stuff off the shelves at the grocery store. They want to touch the pretty glass decorations at your neighbor's house. They ask questions: What is that? Who is that? What is that sound? What is that smell? How long until we get there? They "get into" stuff and can, if misunderstood, annoy their caregivers to no end. Young children, like babies and toddlers, are naturally interested in their surroundings. Without this driving curiosity, without this innate need to explore and understand what the environment provides, children would fail to thrive and to learn. Their ability to make connections and sense of their world would be jeopardized and it is plausible to say that their development would be compromised.

As parents, it is critical that we recognize the role of curiosity in shaping our children's lives. We must respect this innate characteristic by responding to our children positively when they seek to learn. They should not be punished for touching things in their own home or even a home they are visiting. They should not be scolded for being creative with the things they find, like taking all the Kleenexes out of the box and tossing them into the air, watching them fall like little parachutes. They should not be reprimanded for doing what they were created to do, which is to explore their surroundings. Constant parental utterings of "No, no, no." can be confusing to a child. When they gravitate to something of interest, it is far better for parents to follow their child and work with them to explore the newfound interest. Whether it is a plant, a plastic bowl, the remote control, or a silky scarf, talk to your child about what she is seeing and what she is feeling. Describe it to her using rich and vibrant language. Touch it with her. Make relevant associations and pave the way for her to make connections between what she found and the larger world. Validate her interest and in doing so you are teaching your child about the immediate world in which she lives and inevitably building upon her developing language skills. Now, honestly, isn't that more fun than resorting to "No, no. Don't touch."?

If there are specific things that you value in your home and would rather your young child not handle, then put them away for the time being or in a place that is out of your child's reach. Don't allow things in your home to hold more value than your own child's growth and development.

There will come a time when your children are able to understand that something is valuable to you or your family and you would appreciate it being respected as such, but expecting this from a toddler, a preschooler, or even a young child is unfair, and to keep it within reach is just setting them up for failure. Remember that children are mono-focused beings with an amazing ability to zero in on one thing that intrigues them in some way. Take advantage of the opportunity to teach, to lead, to enhance their understanding. When our children are young, we have so many opportunities to explore alongside them, to inspire, to excite, and to enrich. If your child is constantly moving in the direction of something he has been told to stay away from, then his curiosity has not been fulfilled. It's that simple. He's not being defiant, like I've heard so many people claim. A child's interest in his environment is limitless and natural.

Still not sure what to do when little Sally heads towards the bookshelf again? Seize the moment. Communicate. Tell her what she is seeing. Play with it, tap it, and touch it with her. Does the object make a strange sound if you tap on it? Does it feel hot or cold, soft or hard, squishy or bumpy? Can you find another use for it? Would it be safe to pull it off the shelf and allow her to play with it on the floor? The more children are allowed to "play" with the things in their immediate environment to satisfy their curiosities, the less likely they are to randomly grab and pull things in new environments. However, if children are scolded or struck for touching something in their own home and no longer gravitate towards the object, it does not mean that they really understand why they shouldn't touch it. Instead, they just associate the object with pain or discomfort and are deprived of a chance to learn and expand their knowledge.

Children beckon us to teach them about what they see, what they hear and what they feel. A child's interest in his environment is limitless and most importantly, natural. To continually ask a child not to touch things in his world is like telling a starving man not to feast on the food laid before him. It would behoove us, as parents, to become more accepting of our child's need to learn through exploration. If we work to stay involved with our kids instead of working to deter their curiosity it may help us to become a bit more curious too.

Parenting Resources

Books

Unconditional Parenting, by Alfie Kohn

"One basic need all children have, Kohn argues, is to be loved unconditionally, to know that they will be accepted even if they screw up or fall short. Yet conventional approaches to parenting such as punishments (including 'time-outs'), rewards (including positive reinforcement), and other forms of control teach children that they are loved only when they please us or impress us. Kohn cites a body of powerful, and largely unknown, research detailing the damage caused by leading children to believe they must earn our approval. That's precisely the message children derive from common discipline techniques, even though it's not the message most parents intend to send." (Amazon.com)

Playful Parenting, by Lawrence J. Cohen

"From eliciting a giggle during baby's first game of peekaboo to cracking jokes with a teenager while hanging out at the mall, *Playful Parenting* is a complete guide to using play to raise confident children. Written with love and humor, brimming with good advice and revealing anecdotes, and grounded in the latest research, this book will make you laugh even as it makes you wise in the ways of being an effective, enthusiastic parent." (Amazon.com)

Connection Parenting, by Pam Leo

This book is "based on the parenting series Pam Leo has taught for nearly 20 years. Pam's premise is that every child's greatest emotional need is to have a strong emotional bond with at least one adult. When we have a bond with a child we have influence with a child. Pam teaches us that when we strengthen our parent-child bond we meet the child's need for connection and our need for influence." (Amazon.com)

The Natural Child, by Jan Hunt

"In this insightful guide, parenting specialist Jan Hunt links together attachment parenting principles with child advocacy and homeschooling philosophies, offering a consistent approach to raising a loving, trusting, and confident child. *The Natural Child* dispels the myths of 'tough love,' building baby's self-reliance by ignoring its cries, and the necessity of spanking to enforce discipline. Instead, the book explains the value of extended breast-feeding, family co-sleeping, and minimal child-parent separation." (Amazon.com)

Parenting for a Peaceful World, by Robin Grille

This "is a fascinating look at how child-rearing customs have shaped societies and major world events. It reveals how children adapt to and are influenced by different parenting styles and how safeguarding their emotional development is the key to creating a more peaceful, harmonious, and sustainable world." (Amazon.com)

Nonviolent Communication, by Marshall B. Rosenberg

"In this internationally acclaimed text, Marshall Rosenberg offers insightful stories, anecdotes, practical exercises and role-plays that will dramatically change your approach to communication for the better. Discover how the language you use can strengthen your relationships, build trust, prevent conflicts and heal pain." (Amazon.com)

The Five Love Languages, by Gary Chapman

"In *The Five Love Languages*, Dr. Gary Chapman talks about how different people express love in different ways. Some people are verbal, expressing their love in words. Others may never speak their affection, yet they show it by the things they do. Sadly, many couples look to receive love the same way they give it, misunderstanding their spouses. This can lead to quarrels, hurt feelings, and even divorce. However, if you understand each other's love languages, you can learn to give and receive love more effectively." (Amazon.com)

Websites

NaturalChild.org, from their About Us page, "Our vision is a world in which all children are treated with dignity, respect, understanding, and compassion. In such a world, every child can grow into adulthood with a generous capacity for love and trust. Our society has no more urgent task." This website is a wealth of articles ranging on such topics as Gentle Guidance, Living with Children, and Life Learning.

JoyfullyRejoycing.com is a site about peaceful parenting and unschooling. "But overall it's about living more joyful family lives. If I had to summarize it the message would be 'Put the relationship first and then figure out how to fit everything else around that.'"

DrMomma.org, from their Facebook page, "Peaceful Parenting is essentially the effort to mother and father our babies and children in a manner that leads to their optimal health, happiness, and well-being. Peaceful parenting is as old as humanity itself, and is coherent with listening to our own mothering and fathering instincts, as well as tuning into the cues our little ones provide for us. As parenting that is normal, natural, primal and innate, it is *not* exactly the same as the pop-culture definition of 'attachment parenting' and it is *not* a set of hard, fast methods or laws to follow. Peaceful parenting does no intentional harm. It is parenting based not only in natural human and mammalian experience, but also in hard science and evidence-based research."

Parental-Intelligence.com is a parenting and alternative education newsletter published biweekly by unschooling dad, Bob Collier.

Afterword
Skyler J. Collins, Editor

Ahh, you have arrived! Wonderful! And now the fateful question, where do you go from here? You may decide this book is complete hogwash and toss it out the window. Or you may decide that this book is on to something. Realizing, too, that it created more questions than it was willing to answer. That's a good thing! But now what? First things first.

As was explained in the introduction, "what is herein presented is merely the tip of the proverbial iceberg. It's what's under the water that is truly fascinating and life changing." And what better way to discover it than by consulting each resource? The Internet contains a vast and growing archive of free libertarian and voluntaryist thought. Many of the recommended books can be found in electronic format and had for free. You must set off to *develop* your understanding of voluntaryism. But you must also simultaneously set off to *live it*.

And the best place to start is with yourself. Commit never to initiate aggression against another human being; never to coerce someone else against their will; never to pillage, rape, or murder. Recognize that you simply don't have a right to force someone else to do something that they don't want to do. You must use persuasion. If persuasion fails, then that is that. And further, never send an agent to pillage, rape, or murder on your behalf, never send the State to use violence in your stead. If you want to build an art museum, then work a fundraising campaign and seek *voluntary* donations. If the only way to get your art museum is to steal the necessary funds, then it's quite obvious that the art museum shouldn't be built.

The next step is to commit yourself to bettering your approach to and relationship with your children. Think of them as they are, little *people*, with every right that you have. And ask yourself, "How can our relationship develop on the basis of love and trust? How can I be their *mentor*?" Forget immediately this idea that children "behave" one way or another. What may seem like "bad" behavior is really no such thing. It's a yearning to have one's needs met. Children don't "ask" for punishments, they petition for help!

Further, if one is to understand and cherish genuine learning, one must be given genuine liberty to learn. Children have a fundamental right and a natural desire to control their own education. Their curiosity is seemingly infinite, but compulsory schooling quickly destroys that curiosity. Children need freedom over their minds if they are to truly discover and learn anything of real value to themselves; if they are to make sense of the world in a meaningful way. True learning can't be forced. Research unschooling via the provided resources; believe it, implement it, and then you'll see it. Your children deserve no less.

All in all, we can't expect others to change before we change ourselves. Peace and prosperity begins when you realize that *you are already free*, that the world is your playground and your research center, and that *you can do whatever you damn well please*. Sure, there will be obstacles and challenges, but nothing so onerous that they cannot be overcome. If you must use counter-economic means, so be it. Manage such a risk as you manage any other risks in life.

You are free when you take back your freedom. Life is yours to own, happiness is yours to pursue, and allow your children the same privilege. Once again, Godspeed!

Topical Guide

Topic..Chapter

Agorism..3, 12, 16
Arguments for Voluntaryism 1, 3, 6
Behaviorism.. 24, 26, 27, 28, 29, 30
Black/Gray Markets 12, 16
Bullying...24, 25, 26
Central Economic Planning 13, 14, 15
Charity/Welfare.. 1, 6
Child Abuse 24, 25, 26
Church & State 9, 10
Civil Religion 9, 10
Commerce...7, 11, 12, 16
Constitutionalism..4, 9
Counter-Economics... 16
Crony Capitalism (Corporatism) 13, 14
Curiosity of Children..20, 21, 30
Democracy... 1, 4
Economics 3, 11, 12, 13, 14, 15
Free Market 11, 12, 13, 14, 16
Law/Legislation.. 1, 2, 4
Market Process 11, 12, 13
Nonviolent Resistance 3, 5
Parental Influence 21, 23, 24, 25, 26, 29
Peaceful Protest.. 5, 16
Political Labels 2
Public/Compulsory Schooling 17, 18, 19, 24
Punishment of Children...25, 26, 29
Religious Tolerance 7, 8, 9
Socialism... 13, 14, 15
Statism 4, 13, 14, 15
Taxation 1, 4, 14, 15
Unschooling.. 19, 20, 21, 22, 23
Welfare State 4, 14, 15
War 4, 5, 25

About the Editor

Skyler J. Collins lives with his beautiful wife and two wonderful children in Salt Lake City, Utah. He's a devout Latter-day Saint (a Mormon), a voluntaryist libertarian, and an unschooler. He enjoys blogging and reading about anything on liberty, economics, philosophy, religion, science, health and childhood development. He and his wife are committed to raising their children in peace and love, exploring the world with them, and *showing* them how to deal with others respectfully, and enjoy their freedom responsibly.

He is the founder of Everything-Voluntary.com. His websites also include skylerjcollins.com, LibertySearch.info, and LibertyRage.com.

Made in the USA
Lexington, KY
08 June 2012